HOPSCOTCH DAYS

A Remembering of the Way It Was

Beverley Wood

Hopscotch Days
A Remembering of the Way It Was
Copyright © 1999 by Beverley Wood

Cover Design by
Ken Debono

Book Design and Printing by
FALCON BOOKS
San Ramon, California

ISBN   0-9670971-0-X

BeeJay Enterprises
Publisher
623 Rhebas Way
Ridgecrest, CA 96555

PRINTED IN THE UNITED STATES OF AMERICA

For all the real people who live in these pages, who have shared their lives with me (whether willingly or not) and have thereby enriched my life beyond measure.

Contents

PREFACE

This is a true story. Or as true as remembering from a distance can be. Different people remember different things, and these are the things I remember. They happened sixty years ago, two generations ago, in a time so very different from today that it needs to be remembered in some way besides history books.

Some people might call that time a bad time. It was a time of mass poverty and mass unemployment. One terrible war just fading into uneasy memory, the unimaginable prospect of another rumbling like thunder on the horizon. Still, for ordinary people it was a good time.

It was a simpler time, a simpler way of life. Simpler, more naïve, unsophisticated. It was a time when nobody talked about family values; they just had them. Ethics and morals weren't words in a sermon, they were the right way to live. Brotherly love, tolerance, caring—my parents didn't talk about those issues. They didn't have to, they just did them.

People were people, of course, in those times as well as now. Some were fine, others not so fine. By and large most people were too busy surviving to have much patience for wrong-doers. The rule was, you worked hard and did right and that was that. If you did those things you were able to take care of your family, and in those times that was a very difficult thing to do. When you were able to accomplish that without whining, you had great pride and self respect, which were a lot more important than wealth and leisure. "Making do" was the challenge of everyday life; if you could "make do" until payday (stretch the food, wear the old shoes, patch the coat) you could hold up your head and be proud that you didn't have to ask for help.

Families were stable. They did things together at home—they couldn't afford to go out. Amusements were simple—a deck of cards or a library book was an evening's entertainment. Children were secure. They knew their father would bring home some money and that their mother would manage with whatever he brought home. They went to school to learn because they had to, and the teacher was right. There was order and purpose in their days. They knew what to expect and what was expected of them. They had the whole world on a string. They could accomplish anything, because they didn't know they couldn't. It was a good time. I had a good time. This is my story of that time.

January, 1998
Beverley Wood
Ridgecrest, California

CHAPTER ONE

THE FAMILY CIRCLE

I have no idea whether the fact that I was born in 1929 had anything to do with the depression, but certainly the depression had little to do with me. Fortunate we were, surely, to have money coming in regularly (albeit a very little) and a solid roof over our heads, but our real fortune lay in the love and happiness that filled our little house and overflowed into the happy world as seen through childish eyes. As a child I was unaware of the misery and anxiety that lay close about me, for that reality was kept at bay by loving parents. Such protectiveness might be viewed as a mistake, a lack of facing grim reality. As an adult I now know that love, goodness and joy in living as emphasized by my parents are at least as real as pain and unhappiness. I am beginning vaguely to understand the unstinting labor my parents went through to feed and clothe a family of six in those hard times, but how they nourished our hearts, sheltered our happiness, and ensured our morality, from what reservoirs of strength they drew their love and determination and values, only God knows.

My home was full and running over, of love and of people, but I didn't know our tiny house was crowded. Seemed just cozy to me. It was a nice house, I thought—just right. Nobody suggested that the rooms were small; they were just the right size to hold all of us and all of our things. It was a friendly little house and different from any other house on our block. It looked different, and it had different things in it.

On the outside it was covered with brown shingles, and the wooden trim was painted white. That was very different, for most of the houses on our block were white or yellow and made of narrow boards laid down on their sides or covered with pale stucco.

Our windows were different, too. Mama loved plenty of light and sunshine, and so when they bought the little house the first thing Daddy did was to remodel all the windows, making them what Mama called "French" windows. He took the ordinary windows out, made bigger holes and put in tall, thin windows with many panes. Even a very little person could easily look out of those low windows. They opened outwards, and were held open by long hooks which fit into round screw eyes on the window frame. The screens were on the inside of the windows. You could put your tongue against the screen (when nobody was looking to say something about flies and germs) and taste the funny, musty, metallic taste of the wire. Little girls shouldn't lean against the screens or they would make them sag in the frames, and then Daddy would have to take the screen out with a sigh and stretch it tight again.

The front door was all glass panes just like the windows. Mama hung a "glass curtain" over the door—a long, thin, lacy curtain, fastened with a rod at top and bottom to keep it from swinging out as the door opened and closed. Right beside the living room door was the telephone stand Junior had made at school. (My oldest brother was named after Daddy, so his real name was Lewis, but we all called him Junior until far beyond the time he wished we wouldn't.) That telephone stand never held the telephone, because our phone was fastened on the wall, but Mama treasured the stand. Even though I admired it, I disliked it heartily, because its fancy curved wooden legs had to be dusted thoroughly with an oiled cloth in the hands of a little girl—me.

Next to the telephone stand (which in our house held the dictionary) was the door to the boys' room, and next to it was a bookcase with doors. The shelves of the bookcase, besides books, held two treasures I dearly loved. One was a smooth, rounded, speckled shell that, when held to your ear, made a noise like the sea. It was like magic, and it happened every single time. Sometimes I would sneak up on the shell and lift it quickly to my ear to see if I could catch it napping, but I never did; the ocean waves were caught inside somehow. The other special treasure in the bookcase was an amazing make-believe pretzel, about eight inches across. It was made out of some sort of composition material and tinted a toasty yellow and brown just like a real pretzel, with the most convincing little crystals of make-believe salt all over the top. I've no idea where the pretzel ever came from (or why!), but it fascinated me and I never gave up taste-testing the make-believe salt crystals to see if they were real.

Near the bookcase sat Mama's wooden rocking chair with a cushion and a comforting squeak in the rockers. I loved that squeak. Sometimes things happen in a little girl's life that make her want Mama's lap. When the world got too hard for me (and most of those times were my own fault), we would crowd into that chair together. My legs dangling off her lap, I could surreptitiously brush off tears against the front of her clean, starched apron and listen to that comforting squeak while she rubbed my back.

The living room couch, or day-bed as it was called, seemed to me a truly miraculous invention. If you reached under the cloth skirt of the couch cover, you could pull on a handle and out came another part the same size as the couch. That made the whole thing almost as big as a double bed. This was where our company could sleep. Usually our company was various aunts and uncles when they stayed with us instead of at the Big House (which was Grandma's and Grandpa's house in Lemon Grove). Later it was used as a spare bed when my big sister Thelma brought her husband Van to see us (although Mama never believed he really was), or when my brother George brought his wife Alice (who really was, although Mama wished she wasn't).

On the wall above the day-bed was a wooden shelf that Daddy had made to display some of Mama's treasures. Nobody ever had more interesting things on a shelf in their living room. On ours was a little sailboat made of shiny metal, a present for Mama from Junior and George. The most enchanting thing about the sailboat was that it sailed on a little oval mirror for an ocean. On the shelf beside the sailboat was a mysterious Oriental figure wearing a kind of red pajamas. It squatted in a very uncomfortable position holding in its lap a little pot in which you were supposed to burn a tiny cone of incense. It was called an incense burner and the smell of the smoldering incense was supposed to be pleasant. I never liked that figure very much, but I treated it with wary respect for I didn't trust it, and thought the smell of incense was very much over-rated. I was proud of it, though, and showed it off as one of the major attractions of my home. Nobody else I knew had an incense burner. Or a silver boat that sailed on a mirror ocean.

Beyond the day-bed was the most wonderful feature of the living room, the radio. By the time I was born, my family had advanced beyond the very early kind of radio with glass tubes full of bubbling stuff—as I heard my brothers telling about. The first radio I remember was little and sat on a table; it had a domed top and fancy cut-outs in front. Then we got a truly magnificent radio, so big that it stood right on the floor and came up to my chin. It was made of shiny varnished wood, with knobs and a whole row of push-buttons of some new material called plastic. The top of this radio was flat instead of rounded, and it always wore a fancy scarf of black and gold cloth that Daddy had bought in China when he was in the Navy. The black and gold threads of the scarf were woven into pictures and the ends hung down loose in a long fringe.

Near the radio was Daddy's rocking chair. There was no cushion and no squeak in Daddy's chair, and Daddy's lap wasn't soft and comfortable like Mama's. Bony or not, his lap was a good, safe place to be, especially when things were scary. Daddy sat there to listen to the news and to "Baby Snooks" and "Lone Ranger" and "Gang-Busters." I wasn't allowed to listen to "Gang Busters," because they used words like "kill" and "murder," which Mama and Daddy considered bad for children. I thought "Baby Snooks" was just plain silly, but "Lone Ranger" we all liked. I was allowed to sit by the radio in Daddy's chair to listen to "Little Orphan Annie" and "Jack Armstrong" because nobody else liked to hear them. In fact, because "Jack Armstrong" was on just at supper time, and because the rest of my family strongly objected to hearing Jack's adventures with their meal, I was allowed to have my supper on a little table right in front of the radio—probably the first TV dinner ever eaten.

The inside walls of our house were of boards that had been textured with paint mixed with sand, so that (hopefully) they would look somewhat like plastered walls. The floors were of painted boards, with "Congoleum rugs" covering the middle. When we bought them the rugs were rolled up in big stiff rolls and I always thought they would never flatten out when they were brought home and rolled out on the floor, but they always did. They were printed with fancy borders around the edge and patterns in the middle and I thought they were much nicer than fuzzy carpets. They were hard and slick and Mama could sweep and mop and wax them. You could slide on them in your sock feet, you could sit on them and play with your blocks, or you could play with your ball and jacks. They were cool in the summer and felt good to bare feet. Every couple of years we would make a trip downtown to pick out new rugs. How

Mama loved to pick them out. She looked at each pattern and color, and the salesman had to partly unroll each one so that she could stand on it and see how it looked under her feet. It took a long time, and sometimes the salesman would begin to fidget and Daddy would have to glare at him behind Mama's back

Our dining room was the other half of the living room and was separated from the living room not by a wall and a door but by long curtains hung on a black iron rod with round black iron rings. The only times the curtains were pulled shut were when we had company sleeping on the day-bed in the living room, or at Christmas when they were pulled together and kept shut with a clothespin to give Santa Claus privacy. Our dining room table was heavy and round with one center leg that went down to feet that looked like a lion's paws. When there was company we put in a leaf and made the table bigger. Sometimes when it rained Mama would let me put a blanket over the table and make a pretend cave underneath to play in. The whole world looked different from my cave underneath the table. I could see people's feet when they walked past and I could be quiet and they wouldn't even know I was there until I growled and scared them.

When we weren't eating, Mama put a different kind of cloth in the middle, just to look pretty. Once, after Thelma grew up and moved away, she came back with a present for Mama. It was a little square of flowered cloth and a pretty pink bowl, and she showed Mama how to fix the table in the latest style. Thelma laid the square cloth out flat and smooth on the table. Then she set the bowl right in the middle, pressed down and turned the bowl around. As she turned the bowl, the middle of the cloth turned with it but the corners stayed in place, so the bowl was magically surrounded with a pretty swirl of gathers radiating out from the center. Every time I cleared off the table and wiped it clean after meals, I was allowed to arrange the cloth and the bowl just like Thelma showed us. I was proud of the stylish way our table looked between meals. But our table wasn't just for eating on or looking at or playing under. It was for frosting cookies and coloring pictures and doing schoolwork and playing games and making jig-saw puzzles and writing letters. It was a useful and friendly table.

In the winter time the stove that heated our house stood in one corner of the dining room. It was a little round black metal stove with a long shiny pipe that carried the smoke away and outside the house. Mama kept the stove clean and shining. It sat on a special little step in the corner, with a metal tray under it to keep the floor clean, just in case wood or ashes spilled out. I was never allowed to touch the stove, even when I thought it wasn't hot (because some day it might be). In another corner was Mama's sewing machine. It was a beautiful machine, and I was proud of it. I was proud of Mama too, when she sat pushing the treadle so fast with her feet, up and down, and guiding the cloth under the shining needle. I loved to feel the smoothness of the black metal with its fancy gold designs, but I hated the wrought iron curlicues that made the two wide legs and the broad foot treadle. Those had to be dusted every week with an oily cloth, and you had to wrap the cloth around your finger and wipe it in every single hole. Mama would look to see if I missed any holes, and I almost always did, no matter how hard I tried.

High up on the wall beside the door to the kitchen hung the telephone. I wasn't allowed to talk on it very often; it was just for grownups. Only on special occasions or to talk to Grandma or Grandpa could I pull a chair over beside the wall and stand up on it, holding the receiver gingerly to my ear and craning my neck to "talk right into the mouthpiece, dear." Whenever the phone rang, no one was allowed to answer except Mama (or Daddy when he was home). When she answered, we would all stand around and pester her to death asking, "Who is it?" and "What do they want?" We were so curious we couldn't stand to wait, because the telephone was special in those days. Finally, when she couldn't stand our questions while she was trying to talk, Mama would have to leave the receiver hanging down on its cord and frown at us and "shoosh" us away. One day she got so exasperated with our questions that she finally snapped, "That was Mrs. G. and she wanted Daddy's brassiere pattern." After a stunned silence, Thelma and the boys looked at each other and began to splutter and giggle, but they had to explain the joke to me. I was so little I didn't know what a brassiere was or why Daddy probably wouldn't have one. Ever after, in our family, if one of us didn't want to talk about a phone call, our answer was: "It was just Mrs. G. wanting to borrow Daddy's brassiere pattern."

Beyond the doorway into the kitchen was a cupboard that Daddy built from the floor to ceiling. The doors on the top had glass fronts, and there we kept our dishes and glasses. My blue Shirley Temple glass was there and my white cereal bowl with a picture of Babe Ruth in red in the bottom. And I had, all my own, a special spoon with a fancy handle. One time when I was visiting Grandma and Grandpa at the Big House in Lemon Grove, I went with Grandpa to help him get the mail from the mailbox by the front gate. We walked down the path and he lifted me up to open the mailbox. Inside was a long thin white package and he let me carry it in the house to Grandma. When she opened it, she found a beautiful teaspoon. It was what she called a "sample" and it was free, to show people what the pattern was like in case they wanted to buy some. Grandma didn't want to buy any, and she let me keep the sample for myself because I got it out of the mailbox.

Most of our dishes didn't match; in fact, I didn't know they should. It was more interesting to have different kinds.

Some of the dishes came in boxes of oatmeal or soap powder. It was exciting to open a box and see whether you got a cup or saucer or little bowl. Sometimes at the movies they had what was called "Dish Night" when every lady that came to the movie was given a plate or cup. Mama always wanted to get a whole set that matched, but before we could get all of them, they would always change the design.

The kitchen was one of the few rooms in our house that didn't have a tall French window. There wasn't room. The kitchen window was a little one and it was over the stove. Mama longed for a window over the sink so she could look outside when she was doing the dishes, but the sink and sinkboard were opposite the window and all she had to look at while she did dishes was the wall. There were cupboards over the sink and some underneath as well, where Thelma tried to hide the dirty pans when it was her turn to do the dishes (but Mama always caught her). Between the end of the sinkboard and the dining room door was the "cooler." The cooler was a tall cupboard that didn't have a solid floor in it; it was open all the way to the ground, down right through the floor of the house, and was only closed off from the ground underneath by a wire screen. All the shelves in the cooler were made of screen and it had a solid door on the front. Our house was built up on a foundation, not on cement like most houses are built now. There was only air under the floor of the house, and because the air was shaded by the house, it was always cool there, even in the summer. The cool air could come up into the cooler through the screen and circulate through the screen shelves and keep food nice and cool. Butter and fruit and vegetables and eggs and cheese would keep very nicely in the cooler, but meat and milk would have to be kept on ice.

All of that was on one side of the house. On the other side were the bedrooms. At the front of the house, was the boys' room. It had bunk beds with a real ladder (of which I was horribly envious), and a dresser, and two French windows, one on the front and one on the side, and that's all. I made the beds every day, smoothing the sheets and shaking the pillows and tucking in the bright "Indian blankets" that they used instead of bedspreads. I had to be sure to get the sheets smooth and brush out the cracker or popcorn crumbs (they liked to eat and read in bed). For doing that, Junior and George each gave me a dime every week.

My room was next. My room had two doors, one to the dining room and one to the bathroom, and it had one French window. I loved my window best of all, for it looked out at the side yard, where my yard toys were and the pepper tree with my sandbox underneath it. It was a good window. It was a good room, too. Beside the bathroom door was my closet. Instead of a door there was a long curtain of flowered material across the top of the closet doorway. The rod where my dresses hung was behind the curtain and was low so I could reach it. I had boxes underneath where I kept my toys and doll clothes, and shelves on top where Mama kept things I didn't need all the time, like sweaters and galoshes. Along the wall by the window were my doll crib and doll cradle that Daddy had made for me, my wooden table and two chairs, and my little doll house with tiny furniture and tiny dolls in it. These dolls were "doll-house" dolls, to distinguish them from the bigger "real" dolls. My best and newest dolls were kept in my bedroom; the older ones lived outdoors in my playhouse.

Next to my room was the bathroom. It was a nice bathroom, with a little bathtub and a cupboard for towels, and a high window, and a shiny gray painted floor. Daddy painted the floor every year. Before he started painting, he would ask everybody if they were "all through" in the bathroom. Then he would begin to paint the thick enamel on with a big brush, starting at the doorway between the bathroom and my bedroom. Always brushing the same direction, he would paint all around the toilet and around the edges and behind the doors, backing up toward the other doorway. And always, as he worked, we would all find out we just had to "go" and would try to tiptoe in on the unpainted places before he got it all done. Of course, he would have to go back and paint over our footprints. When the paint was partly dry, he could lay down two long, wide boards to walk in on, propped up with a little block of wood at the toilet. In those days, paint took a long time to dry, and Mama always was disappointed that her freshly painted bathroom floor had little tiptoe marks in the paint.

Before we got the hot water heater, Mama had to heat water for our baths in kettles on the kitchen stove. I would sit shivering in the bathtub in an inch of lukewarm water, waiting for Mama to come in with a kettle of hot water, so I would have enough water to wash in. While she poured the hot water in one end, I would have to scrunch up at the other end and stir the water frantically to keep from freezing in spots and boiling in others. Later Daddy installed a little hot water heater in the corner of the bathroom so we could take baths without Mama having to heat all the water on the stove. It was so nice to turn on the taps just right and sit comfortably while the warm water ran in. For a long time we used Lifebuoy soap, which was pretty and smelt interesting and looked like it would taste good, but it didn't. Then Ivory soap came along and that was fun. I spent more time in the bathtub floating the soap than washing with it. Because I was the youngest, I took my bath first. George was next and he would complain bitterly that the soap was soft and mushy by the time I was through with it.

Beyond the bathroom on that side of the house, and beyond the kitchen on the other side and all across the end was one big room that Daddy built when I was born. He and Mama called it the "sleeping porch." Near the kitchen door was the ice box where we kept the milk and meat and other things that needed more cold than the cooler in the kitchen. Inside the icebox was a place to put a block of ice and under the ice was a little hole to drain away the water as the ice melted. The water ran into a pan underneath the icebox and we had to remember to empty it whenever it was full or it would run over and get the floor all wet. You had to get out of the way fast when the iceman came hurrying up the back steps carrying the heavy block of ice in his big shiny tongs. Sometimes he had to chip a little off the edges to make the block fit and then there were chips of slippery ice to suck.

Next to the icebox was the back door that led outside to the cement steps where I liked to play jacks, and down the steps was the back yard. On the other end of the sleeping porch, behind a partition, was where Mama and Daddy slept. There was their big double bed, where I could go if I had a bad dream in the night. There was their closet where their clothes hung, Mama's flowered dresses and Daddy's fireman uniforms with gold braid and shiny brass buttons. When I was very little I slept in my crib out there while Thelma slept in the bedroom that became mine when I got bigger. That was before she got tired of being a girl at home and went away to be a grownup. That was our house. It was pretty and friendly and safe, and inside of it lived our family.

Our family started first with Mama and Daddy. Love, I have found, doesn't always choose a convenient time to tie two hearts together and it doesn't see into the dim future and warn, "Be careful—hard times are coming." That was the kind of love that changed the future of a most unlikely couple in 1914. Daddy was Lewis then. Raised on a worn-out Illinois farm, the middle child of five, he had to leave school at the end of the fifth grade because it was too far to walk to school without shoes and his widowed mother couldn't afford to buy them. Lewis listened to trains going past to somewhere else, and read everything he could find to read about the world, and he dreamed of adventure. When his mother at last remarried, Lewis was free to "run away to sea." After eight years in the Navy, he decided it was time to seek his fortune, and he chose sunny San Diego to do it in. With his savings he bought an automobile and began to work as a "jitney bus" driver. That was the same thing as a taxi, but they were called jitney buses because it cost a "jitney" (which was a nickel) to ride in one. His job was to drive tourists south across the Mexican border to the town of Tijuana, and back again. Lewis took people other places, too, and one day he picked up a new passenger outside Normal School and took her back to her home in Lemon Grove. On that trip his life was forever changed, for that passenger was a dainty bit of femininity with a crown of honey-blonde hair, a soft sweet mouth, and an irresistibly tip-tilted nose. That was Mama when she was Ruth.

Ruth's Mama and Papa noticed that the same car brought her home each time, and finally her Mama told her with a sigh, "Ruth, you might as well ask him in so we can all meet him." So she did. Lewis was past his first youth by that time, but he was a handsome, upstanding young man. He had a ruddy face and keen blue eyes that held a twinkle of dry humor. His square jaw and determined mouth almost disguised his natural gentleness, but not quite. In spite of his having been in the Navy, his manners were above reproach, and it didn't take long for him to make friends with Ruth's parents and many brothers and sisters. They all liked him and he liked all of them, but Lewis liked Ruth best and they were soon married.

Ruth had never been far from home, and she was never to be very adventurous, but wherever he went, there she followed (like her namesake Ruth in the Bible). Packing for their honeymoon meant loading his car with tent and blankets besides all her worldly possessions, for they were heading north to find a likely place to settle and buy some land for a little farm. Grandma wasn't too pleased that they moved up north right after they were married, but off they went.

They had a fine trip, except for a few excitements. After a long day of driving, one camp site they chose in a secluded woods was suddenly and inexplicably overrun with rowdy pigs, and the bride retreated shrieking inside the tent while her husband, trying not to laugh, chased the pigs off with a stick. One evening near Shasta, they determined to jump in the river for a bath. As it turned out it was only Lewis who got wet at all, and he leaped out as fast as he leaped in, gasping and blue with cold, and Ruth decided she didn't want a bath in that icy water, after all. Nevertheless, they had a wonderful honeymoon as they made their way north. Coming from the more barren southern California, Ruth had never before seen such big trees, rushing rivers, or lush green growth, and the snapshots she sent home were entitled in her round, careful writing, "Jungle Scenes."

In northern California Lewis worked at a lumber camp while they looked for their land. They lived in a newly built company cabin in beautiful forest surroundings, but life was not all peaches and cream. Burros ate Lewis' socks right off Ruth's clothesline, and the cabin was infested with cockroaches. They tried raising chickens for fresh eggs, but lost most of them to coyotes. Their last surviving chicken, a crippled one which had become a pampered pet, was snatched one day from its pen by a hawk, and although Lewis ran for his gun, he was too late to save their pet. At last, with Ruth feeling ill, and the roaches so thick they gave her nightmares, they sadly (on Lewis' part, at least) postponed their plans for a farm and returned to San Diego to raise their family, which appeared to be well on the way.

First there was Thelma, Mama's and Daddy's first child. She was pretty and dainty and delicate. When she was two years old, Lewis Junior was born, and exactly a year later, George came into the family. When George was a tiny baby, even before he and Mama left the hospital where he was born, he was seriously ill. The doctor told Mama her baby wouldn't live long and she should say good-bye and just leave him in the hospital. Not Mama! She bundled up her sickly little baby and took him right home to the family. He had asthma and pneumonia, and if she laid him down he couldn't breathe. She held him up all the time, loving him and taking care of him. Even when she had to do things for three-year-old Thelma and one-year-old Junior, she still held the baby. Even when she was so tired she was afraid she would go to sleep and drop him, she sat in her rocking chair and held him all night long. To keep from going to sleep, she would hold a book in her free hand and read out loud to him from her grown-up book. And with all the love (and maybe the reading, too), he lived and grew up to be strong and happy and to have a good, long and useful life. Those three little children grew up together and played to- gether and fought together and made a family with Mama and Daddy.

Then ten years after George was born, there was a new baby and that was me. Things were a little different for me because my brothers and sister were so much older than I was. Thelma was thirteen years older, Junior eleven years older, and George (the closest one to me in age) was ten years older. Mama said they spoiled me, but I didn't notice. When I was little, we all lived together like a family should, and that was nice.

Thelma was the oldest, and because she was the big sis- ter, she was sometimes a little bossy. She had pretty blonde hair and wore fluffy dresses and knew how to type and how to sew doll clothes and cut out paper dolls. Because she was almost grown up now she had boyfriends. When I was very little, just a baby, if Mama was busy in the house, she would sometimes put me in my buggy and ask one of the older chil- dren to take me for a walk. They usually had other, important things to do, so Thelma thought of a way to take me for a walk and read at the same time (she loved to read—we all did). We lived on a hill. She would take me in the buggy out to the front sidewalk, and tie a long rope on the handle of the buggy. Then she would sit down on the sidewalk with her book in one hand and the end of the rope in the other. Giving the buggy a push, Thelma would let it roll down the hill until it came to the end of the rope, and then she would haul on the rope until the buggy and I were up the hill again. Back and forth I would go in the buggy having a nice time while she sat and enjoyed her book. Until one day Mama came out looking for us. She didn't like Thelma's good idea very much.

Thelma always had good ideas, I thought. She liked to entertain me when I was little by doing cartwheels, handstands and other extraordinary acrobatic feats (at least, I thought they were extraordinary; our brothers called them "showing off"). When she was about eighteen and old enough to know better, she was busy entertaining me one rainy day by showing me how long she could stand on her head. Choosing the only corner available in the living room —just beside the glass-paned front door—Thelma tucked her dress into her underpants so her skirts wouldn't fall down over her face, and hoisted herself upside down. There she stood, with her legs straight up in the air and her face turning purple, when her current boyfriend stepped up on the front porch to knock on the door. There they stood looking at each other through the glass door, the boyfriend outside standing on his feet, and Thelma inside, standing on her head and trying desperately to pretend she was somewhere and somebody else. I don't know what happened next. I jumped up from the floor and ran away to my bedroom so I could laugh out loud into the pillow.

People always thought my brothers were twins because their birthdays were the same day and they were about the same size, but they were really very different. I thought George was the handsomest and he always treated me nicely, not like a little girl who might be in the way. He bought me licorice with his own money, even when Mama said I shouldn't eat that stuff. Junior liked to tease, but he had the nicest smile and made me laugh. He teased me a lot. He would tell me the reason the breakfast oatmeal was slimy was because there had been snails in it (I detested the slimy creatures), but he would take me to Sunday School on his bicycle. Both of them thought I was pretty cute. I think they were the only ones who ever did, but I didn't argue with them. I was proud to have such a beautiful big sister and two such nice and handsome brothers.

As I grew older, I found that our family was really bigger than just the six of us who lived in our house. Our family included grandparents and aunts and uncles and cousins. One grandmother, who was Daddy's mother, lived a long way from our house. She lived in Illinois, which was "back East," and we saw her only a few times. We wrote to her and sent pictures and presents to her. We got letters back from her that always started the same way, "Dear Son and Family, All fine here and hope you are the same." When I was born she had sent a very special and beautiful quilt that she had made for me. It was much too precious to use every day and it was kept put away and only brought out to put on my bed for a special treat if I was sick-in-bed, and then I had to be very careful not to spill chicken soup on it. I loved my quilt and liked to study each different piece of material that made up the pattern and imagine my little old grandmother putting in the tiny stitches that made the ornate pattern of quilting. That grandmother wasn't real to me until at last we made a trip back East, and then I knew her and she became my Grandma and not just a name on a letter.

My other Grandma and my Grandpa were always real to me, for they lived not very far away in Lemon Grove. This

Grandma and Grandpa were Mama's parents and they had come all the way from Illinois and New York, across the Oregon Trail to raise their growing family in the sunny little valley of Lemon Grove just out of sight and sound of the sea. They lived in the Big House, so called to distinguish it from the Little House. The Big House was (to my eyes at least) a wonderfully roomy two-story house, in a grassy yard set around with orange and lemon trees. There was a little front porch with sunny windows and a wicker chair where Grandpa liked to sit and smoke his pipe. In front of the window on a wicker stand lived the big fern plant that a little girl could look at and even sit under, but mustn't touch.

On the right was the living room (Grandma called it the parlor), which to me seemed dark and uninteresting, and the dining room was on the left. The only interesting thing in the dining room was the picture above the doorway. I coveted that picture. It's a wickedness in me that, after all these years, I continue to covet that picture. It was in a frame almost as wide as the doorway but only about six inches high. Just exactly fitting the frame was the picture of a long tree branch, with a row of adorable fat stodgy little birds sitting shoulder to shoulder all along the branch. Usually I went right through the house to the big, light kitchen at the back of the house, but I would stop briefly to be sure the little row of birds was still roosting there above the dining room door. The kitchen had a big table in the middle and windows all around and a big, dark, good-smelling pantry where Grandma kept her cookie jar. Beyond was the back yard where a little girl could dig in the dirt under the lemon tree all she pleased.

The very best, most special and surprising part of the Big House was to be found on the stairway. Halfway up the staircase that led to the bedrooms, where the stair turned, was a high window set into the wall. Underneath the window on the landing was built a little cushioned bench just big enough for one person and some books. It was such fun to sit there and read, looking down on the household below, hearing faraway talk from the kitchen and smelling the quiet woodsy smell of Grandpa's pipe floating up from the sunny porch. I could sit there all by myself—a princess on a throne, far removed from all my poor subjects below. Until the princess thought about Grandma's cookie jar and abdicated her throne to run down to the kitchen.

That was the Big House where Grandma and Grandpa lived with Mama's youngest sister Adeline. Next door to the Big House and facing the same front yard was the Little House where Mama's brother Edgar and his family lived. We visited all the folks in Lemon Grove often, for it wasn't very far from our house in San Diego. In Mama's whole family of brothers and sisters there were lots of cousins the age of my brothers and sister, so there was almost always someone for them to play with. With there being so many cousins, of course, there were often arguments and disagreements, occasionally riots, and even bloodshed. Then Mama's oldest sister Gladys would hurry out to settle things by calling sweetly in her soft, ladylike voice, "Gently, children, gently!" A sweeter, more gracious lady never lived than my Aunt Gladys, but her way of subduing a yardful of squabbling children never accomplished much except to make them giggle. Actually, her "Gently, children, gently!" probably worked better than anything else, for as Thelma said in later years, they couldn't figure out how to hit each other gently, so they had to stop fighting to laugh!

By the time I came along, all that crowd of cousins had grown older and weren't very pleased to have a little girl tagging along. I desperately wanted a few cousins my own age, but just my luck, when the next cousin after me was born (Adeline's little girl Joan), she turned out to be terminally adorable. Even as a child I knew she was stupendously charming and I, as her older cousin—knobby-kneed, sober, and socially inept—was left in perpetual wonder as to how she did it. She was a fairy. I was more like a skinny little gnome. However, I had no hard feelings. It wasn't her fault; she couldn't help being precociously cute. Despite the difference in ages and charm, we did manage to strike up a relationship, but the fun of having all those same-age cousins to pal around with all summer long eluded both Joan and me.

For years after they first moved to Lemon Grove, Grandma and Grandpa didn't have indoor plumbing; they had an outhouse. It was always kept clean and sweet-smelling, painted white, with the old Sears catalog hanging from a string in the corner. That catalog served two purposes: you could read what was left of it while you sat there, and then you could tear off a page and use it for other things. By the time I can remember, the bathroom was inside the house near the back door. The toilet didn't have a handle to flush with like ours at home. You had to reach up (little people like me had to stand up on the seat to do it) and pull on a thin chain hanging from a big box on the wall. You always expected water to come pouring down out of the box like a waterfall, but all the action happened inside somewhere. It was exciting, and sometimes Mama had to come in and make me stop pulling the chain and listening to waterfalls.

Grandma and Grandpa had to buy their firewood because there was no place nearby where there were any trees for wood. When they first lived there the Indians from Temecula would drive down now and then with a wagonload of firewood to sell. Quite often Indian ladies, or "squaws" as they were then called, would come along too and sell baskets and things. That was when Mama was a little girl, and those squaws thought she was the prettiest little thing with her big blue eyes and long blonde curls. Grandma was just a little afraid of those Indians and always held tightly to her little Ruth while they were there. She was afraid those squaws wanted a little blonde girl to take back home with them. Grandma wasn't afraid, though, of the Chinese man who came around peddling vegetables. He was a nice brown man with a big white smile, and he adored little Ruth. When he pulled his horse up in front of the house with his cart full of fresh vegetables, he would call, "Ruthie, oh Ruthie," and when she came running out he would laugh and search in his pockets for the sweet litchi nuts he had brought for her. She liked the days that Chin Lee came.

It was a busy household when Mama and her brothers and sisters were little. There were eight of them altogether. First was Walter, then Leo and Edgar and Merrill. In-between were two little babies who died. Then came Gladys and Ruth (who was my Mama) and Harry and a long time later, Adeline. Long after all of them were grown up and married and had children, I loved to hear Mama tell stories about that big family and all the funny things they did. They were my favorite stories and I called them Mama's "I'll never forget . . . " stories. When she started out with those words, I would settle down and listen carefully, for they were wonderful tales. With so many children, they often had hard times, but Mama seemed not to remember those times as much as the fun they had being a big family. They usually had enough to eat and clothes to wear and a place to live, so they were all right. None of our relatives ever seemed to get rich, but nobody seemed to worry much about it.

I suppose Mama and Daddy knew we were poor, but I didn't know. How could I? I had everything I needed, so it seemed to me that we were rich. In those days, little girls didn't need much to feel rich. There were Mama and Daddy to take care of me and hug me and kiss me good-night. There was my big sister to help tie my shoes and make doll clothes for me, and there were my big brothers to push me in my swing and play card games with me. There was my own bedroom with my own playthings in it (children didn't call them "toys" in those days). There was a rope swing outside that Daddy had made, a tree to climb in, and right next door lived my best friend to play with.

In the 1930's most people were poor and some were very poor. Daddy had a job, so we weren't so poor as other families. He was a fireman and wore a uniform to work, with brass buttons and gold braid on his coat and cap. On his coat was a badge with a raised pattern of a trumpet-shaped horn on it. To my eyes he was a fine sight, striding so briskly up the street in the morning on his way to the fire station, looking so smart and shiny in his uniform. He had to stay at the fire station for all day and all night, and then he came home for a whole day and night.

Sometimes we visited him at the fire station. Holding Mama's hand, I liked to walk into the big, echoing garage where the shiny red fire engine was waiting, the big hoses neatly coiled up, ready to use if the alarms rang. Daddy showed us the room upstairs where the firemen on duty slept at night in narrow cots. It was a very strange room, I thought, with a round hole in the middle of the floor and a shiny brass pole fastened to the ceiling above and going through that hole clear down to the floor of the garage below where the fire engine waited. Daddy told us how at night the firemen would put their tall rubber boots ready beside their beds, with the bottoms of their pant legs pushed down inside and the tops of the heavy pants folded down just so. If the alarm rang in the middle of the night, the men would jump out of bed and stick their feet down through the pants legs and into the boots all at once. They could pull up their pants quickly and snap the elastic suspenders over their shoulders and be all dressed. Then they would run to the middle of the room and grab that slippery pole, wrap their legs around it and slide right down it—fast! That was much quicker than going down the stairs. It looked like fun, too. I always wanted to try sliding down that pole, but I wasn't allowed to go near it. Mama and I liked to see the little kitchen where the firemen took turns cooking their own meals. It was always very neat and clean, but I thought it was funny to think of all those men cooking for themselves without any ladies around to help them.

Sometimes at home in the middle of the night we would hear the fire alarm ring. By counting the bells, we could usually figure out where the fire was. That alarm in the night, loud in the dark and waking me up, gave me a funny, scary feeling in my middle. Mixed up with that feeling was pride that Daddy was helping save people and their houses. I thought Mama must be proud, too. When that alarm rang on the nights Daddy was working, Mama would get up and put on her bathrobe and sit in the living room. She would sit there alone, rocking in her chair in the dark, just humming softly to herself and listening for the fire engine to come back. I thought Mama was probably remembering a time, many years before I was born, when they carried Daddy home again, limp and smoky and scaring her. Waiting in my warm bed now, I would listen to the creak, creak, creak of the rocking chair in the dark living room. After awhile when the fire engine came back, Daddy would call on the telephone. Then Mama would sigh and climb back into her bed.

Most of the people in my family worked. When they were only little boys, Junior and George delivered newspapers. At first they walked down all those streets, leaving newspapers at the houses on their lists, not forgetting one. Over their shoulders they carried the big heavy gray canvas bags full of folded papers. After awhile they saved enough money to buy bicycles, and then they had bags on the back of their bicycles, one hanging down on each side, to hold the newspapers. The bicycles had little lights on the front and bells to ring when you wanted people to get out of the way. The boys wore thin metal clips like bracelets around their ankles to keep the bottoms of their pants from getting tangled in the bicycle chains. I thought they looked very smart, with their newspaper bags and their bicycles and their shiny clips. Sometimes they would take me for a ride on the back of the bicycle.

I thought it would be fun to ride a "two-wheeler," but I never could learn—not then nor later—although I tried and tried. Thelma always wanted to do everything our brothers did (and better), but she couldn't ride very well, either. The first time she tried it in the back yard on Junior's bicycle, she went too fast and couldn't stop. She ran smack into Daddy's outdoor work bench and bent the front wheel till it was square. When the boys got older and got better jobs, they bought an old car and fixed it up to go places. They didn't take me for rides in the car as much as they had taken me for rides on their bicycles. I guess they didn't have a little sister in mind when they bought the car.

Thelma worked, too. She helped take care of children sometimes, and when she got older she sat in an office and typed and added up long columns of figures. I thought it must have been more fun to take care of the children. Mama and I were the only ones in the family who didn't have real jobs. Mama didn't have time for a job. She worked all day cleaning and washing and ironing and cooking. Every day she swept and mopped the painted wooden floors and the slick Congoleum rugs. She had to do it every day because of George's asthma; he wheezed if there was any dust any- where.

Every single day we all had to wear clean clothes, Mama said so; and every week she washed and starched and ironed all those clothes. Because he had a job, Daddy had enough money to buy her a real washing machine, so she didn't have to rub the clothes on a rough washboard in soapy water like some mothers did. She would wash our clothes in the big round green electric washing machine and put them one by one through the wringer that squeezed the water out of them. The wringer was on top of the washing machine and it was two rubber rollers that rolled toward each other. When they were rolling, they would pull the wet clothes right in between them and out the other side into the clothes basket. They could catch fingers between them if you weren't very careful, and the wringer had a special button to push hard to open up the rollers if that happened. One Christmas, Santa Claus brought me a little tin washing machine that really worked. You could fill it with water and soap and wash doll clothes in it, but it wasn't electric like Mama's. Mine had a little handle that you turned round and round to make the clothes swish back and forth and get clean. It didn't have a wringer, either. I had to squeeze the water out of the clean clothes myself.

When the clean clothes were all wrung out, Mama would carry the basket full of hot, steamy wet things out into the back yard and hang them on the clotheslines. The clotheslines were made of wires strung loosely across the yard, low enough so that she could reach to hang the clothes on them. First she wiped off all the wires with a rag so the dusty wire wouldn't get the clean clothes dirty. Then she fastened the wet clothes on the wire with her wooden clothespins. Mama never left her clothespins on the line when she took down the dry clothes like some ladies did. The clothespins got dirty that way, and she thought that was sloppy (sloppy, to Mama, was a cardinal sin). She kept her clothespins clean in a pretty cloth bag with flowers embroidered on it. The bag had a hook on it and hung on the clothesline so it was handy to get the clothespins out as she needed them.

When she was through hanging up the wet clothes, Mama took the long wooden clothes poles and propped them under the loose wires to raise them high up in the air so while the wet clothes were blowing and flapping and getting dry up high in the breeze, people could walk around in the yard underneath. When the clothes were dry, Mama took them down and sprinkled them with water and rolled them up tight all ready to iron. I thought it was strange to dry the clothes and then wet them again, but that was the way it was done.

Mama's ironing board was a long smooth board, narrower at one end, covered tightly with a piece of blanket and then a white cloth. It didn't have any legs. Daddy had made it just long enough so that the wide end rested on the edge of the kitchen stove and the narrow end rested on the sinkboard, which was exactly the same height as the stove. The irons (there were two) sat on the kitchen stove to heat, and that's why the stove had to be nearby. When one was hot, Mama lifted it with its wooden handle and tested it to be sure it wasn't too hot. To test it, she licked her finger and touched it very quickly to the bottom of the iron. By the way the wetness sizzled, she knew whether it was too cool to iron the clothes, or so hot it would scorch them, or just right. Then she would iron while the other iron was on the stove getting hot. When the first iron was so cool it wouldn't iron the clothes any more, she set it back on the stove and tested the second one. That was how she ironed all those clothes. Mama ironed our clothes that way for years, but Daddy always liked to buy her the newest inventions whenever he could and one day bought her an electric ironing machine called a "mangle." With that machine, she could sit down while she ironed the sheets and pillow cases and tablecloths. Mama even got so expert that she could iron starched white shirts with her mangle.

Our first waffle iron and toaster were like the old irons —they didn't work on electricity, they heated on the stove. They worked very well and Mama made good waffles and toast that way. Then for Christmas one year the boys got Mama a wonderful electric toaster. It was as long as two slices of bread but just as wide as one. It had a lid that lifted up like a waffle iron only it was smooth and flat. You put the bread on the bottom and closed the lid and in a few minutes you lifted the lid and had toast. It squashed the bread a little, but I liked it that way. It did lots of things besides make toast, too. You could make toasted cheese sandwiches in it. You could open the lid all the way down and make a little square griddle that you could fry something on, like bacon and eggs. We took that toaster with us later on one of our trips back East and it worked very well to cook our breakfast or suppers sometimes.

When she wasn't washing, ironing, cleaning or fixing meals, Mama was sewing clothes for us or crocheting or knitting pretty and useful things. She knitted a coat for herself one winter, out of good brown yarn, and she wore that coat for years. When she couldn't mend the holes in the elbows any more, she didn't throw the coat away. Instead, she set to work and unraveled the yarn it was made of. I helped do that and it was fun. If you picked out the right end of yarn, you could pull and it would come undone into one long curly string of yarn. Then Mama cut out and threw away the worn-out parts of the yarn, and before it got tangled up she wound it into big loose rolls. When the coat was all turned into big rolls of yarn, she washed the rolls carefully and hung them up to dry. I helped her wind the dry yarn into fat balls, and then Mama took her knitting needles and made me a pretty new brown winter coat. Nobody could tell it was once Mama's old, worn-out one.

Even though I was the youngest, I did some of the work. I took the big straw broom and swept the porches and sidewalks all around the house. Every morning I made my brothers' beds, and for that they paid me ten cents a week. I dusted the furniture, and that was fun—except for the sewing machine. After supper I dried the dishes as Mama washed them and put them away in the dish cupboard in the dining room. Another one of my jobs was to set the table for supper. First I took off the glass bowl and fringed scarf that Mama kept there when we weren't eating or playing cards. Then I got out the tablecloth and spread it evenly over the table. Then came the plates and the knives and forks and spoons, some on the right and some on the left, with a napkin folded neatly under the fork.

Mama was a good cook, but as she herself said, she was a good "plain cook." Meaning she didn't make fancy dishes, just plain solid substantial good-tasting ones. She would move quickly and lightly back and forth in her tiny, inconvenient kitchen and get a whole meal on the table, everything hot and fresh and ready to eat all at the same time. She could fix better meals for less money than anyone I have ever known, and she was a nutritionist ahead of her time. Before it was popular to do so, she persisted in serving balanced meals. We always had vegetables and cereals and fruits, all the right food groups, even before much was known or said about nutrition and vitamins. None of her recipes were spectacular or particularly memorable. It was her meal planning and timing (to have everything done at once), and the love she served with her meals that made them so satisfying. Supper was a nice time. That was when all the workers were home together again, sitting around the table in the dining room and talking about their day. I liked to listen to my sister and brothers talk and joke together. They had such fun, even when they argued. Sometimes I felt a little left out of their talking and joking, and wished I had known them when they were little like me.

I knew what they looked like when they were little. Daddy had a nice Kodak camera and liked to take pictures and Mama pasted them neatly in her photograph albums. I loved to get out those photograph albums and look at the pictures of everybody. There was a red album and a green one, and both of them were family. The green book had the oldest pictures in it. Those pictures were of Mama and Daddy and their families when they were Ruth and Lewis, before they were married. In that book the ladies wore long dresses and the men all wore ties. There were pictures of Mama when she was a very little girl with long blonde curls and big hair ribbons, with her little brother Harry wearing a dress and his hair in long curls, too (but without the hair ribbon). I thought that was very strange, but that's the way people dressed their little boys when they were very young. In those old pictures, the people's clothes were different and their hair was different and they were much younger, but when I looked in the eyes of those pictured people, I knew them. I could point to a graceful young girl with head tilted to one side and say, "There's Aunt Gladys!" The tall stoop-shouldered man with dark hair and mustache instead of white was most certainly Grandpa. The young man sitting at the wheel of a touring car and wearing a dashing tweed cap was surely Lewis. The oldest picture of all was a crumbling daguerreotype showing Daddy's family while they were still a family, before his father died and left them. On the porch of a tiny wooden house sat a serious young woman (the grandmother I'd never seen) with a baby on her lap; beside her stood the handsome young man who died so young, with the four older children grouped around them. The middle-sized little boy dressed in overalls and looking right into my eyes was Lewis, and that was Daddy.

In those old photos, I loved the way my sweet young mother looked in her long and graceful dresses, with her lovely hair parted softly in the middle and pinned up in a braided coil on the back of her head. There was Daddy, with his hat on just so and very solemn and serious. He always wore a hat if he could, because he lost his hair when he was just a young man. Even when he first met Mama, his reddish hair was very thin on top, and we children never knew him with any hair except for a fringe around the edge. It suited him, though, and we thought he was very handsome. Daddy was short but stocky and strong, and he never gained an ounce of fat. He stood foursquare and looked you directly in the eye, even if you sometimes tried to avoid it.

In the red photograph album the people were more familiar to me. There was Daddy in his fireman's uniform. Here was Mama in an astounding hat and carrying a daintily dressed baby girl who was Thelma. Then there were three little children—a sober little girl with glasses, a lad with big ears and a wide and devilish grin, and a chubby, angelic-looking toddler almost as big as his brother. Then came a medley of aunts and uncles and cousins, and finally me. Me as a curly-haired baby with a ball, me as a hair-ribboned toddler, me with a Christmas tree, me with a Dutch bob, me knobby-kneed in a swimsuit, me with an attitude, me with my family.

Most of the photos of my family show a serious and sober set of people. That isn't our fault; it's due to the way our faces are built. Mama was the only one who could smile. When Daddy smiled, you'd never know it, and we children mostly took after him. When Junior and George took up photography for a hobby (with a darkroom and everything), they tried to take family portraits. Everybody would pose obediently as best they could, but you would hear the boys crying despairingly from behind the camera, "Smile, Dad, smile." "I am," Daddy would protest, amazed. At last, they would have to shout, "Show your teeth, Dad, show your teeth," for that was the only expression that remotely resembled a smile. I don't know why. We were ordinarily perfectly cheerful and happy, but I believe our faces were chipped from good Scotch granite.

No matter what they looked like, no matter how well I knew them or not—all the people in those photograph albums belonged to me. They were mine. It was my own big family circle. I was part of it and I reveled in it.

CHAPTER TWO

WHERE THE HEART IS

Winter was usually a pleasant season where we lived, not too cold, not too wet. Most days it was warm enough for me to play outside, but even in sunny San Diego it rained sometimes. If it didn't rain too hard, I could put on my yellow raincoat and floppy hat, pull on my galoshes and go out to play. It was fun to splash down the long front path, out the gate and down the steps to the sidewalk. In the gutter at the edge of the street a little river of brown water hurried down the steep hill to where the street ended at the bottom. I liked to walk in the gutter in my galoshes clear down to the end of the street, with the water pushing me along. At the bottom all that water rushed through a hole in the street, swirling through the iron grating that covered the hole so nobody could fall in. I could put a little piece of wood in the water at the top of the hill, and race down the hill, trying to beat it to the bottom to watch it tumble through that hole. The way the water swooshed through that grating was scary, for if the bars came off a little girl might be sucked right down into that dark hole, I thought. After watching for awhile, I would turn around and walk back up the gutter, only now instead of going along with me the water was fighting me—pushing against my boots, curling up high and trying to get over the tops. Sometimes if I pushed back hard against the water, it did go right up over the tops of the galoshes. Then my feet in their wet socks sloshed around in the boots like wet fishes and I would have to take my boots off and dump the water out before I could go in the house.

Mama didn't mind so much when I got wet. She just made me take my wet things off and put on dry ones. Mud was a different story. She wasn't very pleased when Daddy helped me make rivers and dams in the mud of our back alley after it rained. We built dams and spillways of rocks and mud and sticks, and he showed me what happened when the dam got too full. When we were finished with our dams, Daddy and I would come back into the yard with mud caked on our hands and arms and legs, and my galoshes so thick and heavy with mud that I could hardly walk. We stood on the back step and called Mama to come out and look at us, and we laughed at her expression when she saw us. Mama made us get the hose and wash off right outside, standing out in the rain and getting even wetter. When all the mud was gone, then we could come in.

Mama would try to look cross at Daddy, but then he would stamp in all wet and cold, and hold his arms out wide to give her a big damp bear hug. She would have to stop frowning then and laugh inside his arms. Plump as she was, she would almost disappear inside that huge hug. "Dearie," he called her, saying, "Dearie, give us a hug." That's what he did every time he came home from work, opening the door and hollering for her and spreading his arms wide to hold her tight. I loved it when Daddy bear-hugged Mama, and I would hurry to them and hug them both as high up as I could reach. Daddy liked to tease Mama, just a little bit, about being plump. He would pretend he couldn't reach around her and then brag that when they were married he could reach around her waist with his hands. If she began looking worried, he would laugh and tell her that now she "was all the more to love."

On rainy days the house was cozy inside, with the rain slanting down outside the tall windows. There would be popcorn to eat and games to play and jig-saw puzzles to make. Daddy didn't like puzzles very much, but the rest of us did. Once we were all (except Daddy) working on a terribly hard new puzzle. All the pieces looked exactly alike and they didn't fasten tightly together; they slid around loosely even when they did match. Mama and Thelma and the boys worked and worked on it, and even I found a few pieces. They got sick and tired of bending over the table, but they were determined to finish it, and finally they had that puzzle almost done. Then Thelma, in a big hurry, tried to put a piece in the wrong place, and when it wouldn't fit, she lost her temper. She got madder than a wet hen and with both hands scattered that poor puzzle all over the table. Junior and George jumped up with a dreadful yell. They rushed around the table and chased Thelma screaming right out of the house into the rain. When the door slammed behind them and I heard Thelma's shrieks, I stood petrified and a little scared. Mama just smiled and began to pick up the scattered puzzle. "Thelma deserves what she gets this time," she laughed.

The wood-burning stove in the corner of the dining room kept our little house nice and warm. We weren't as poor as families whose daddies didn't have a job, but we didn't have money to waste buying wood to burn up in the stove. Wherever Daddy saw a house being built, he would ask permission and then we could go with gunny sacks to pick up chips and scraps of wood to use for kindling. And instead of buying logs to burn, we made our own. I loved to go in the car with Daddy to the lumber mill outside of town. I liked the smell of the wood and sawdust, I liked to see the great piles of tree trunks, and I liked to see the clean, damp, yellow boards after they were sawed from the tree trunks. But I didn't like the noise of the screaming saws when they were making those boards, and I held tight to Daddy's hard, square hand, just in case one of those saws got loose and came after me. Daddy would talk to the foreman, and he would show us where the yellow and brown sawdust was all scraped together in big piles. We weren't allowed to go anywhere else at the lumber yard, but we could scoop our boxes full of the sweet-smelling sawdust. We only took what we needed and left the rest for other people.

When we got home with the sawdust, Daddy spread it out on newspapers in the shed to dry. Then he poured kerosene over it and mixed it up. I didn't like that part very much. I helped stir it up, but the sawdust didn't smell nice any more; it was dark and oily. When the sawdust and kerosene were all mixed up we laid more old newspapers on the cement floor and Daddy put a scoop of the oily sawdust on each one. He rolled and folded the paper tightly around the sawdust, neatly tucking in the last flap so it couldn't unroll. That made a nice clean little log to burn in the stove instead of wood. He showed me how to roll the logs, and even though my hands were so much smaller than his, I was proud that I could make the logs almost as well as he did. When we finished making sawdust logs, we would take an armful into the house and load the wood-box beside the stove and the house stayed nice and warm all winter.

In the winter when the days were short, there wasn't much time to play out-of-doors after school. That was the time for playing games at the round dining room table. Our whole family liked to play cards, and they took care that I should learn to play the games they enjoyed, so even when I was very little I knew how to play grown-up games. They never played baby games with me and they never let me win on purpose. We played Rummy and Hearts and Casino and Cribbage. Thelma knew how to play lots of different kinds of Solitaire and she taught me how to play all of them so I could even play cards by myself if nobody else was around. My friends didn't know how to play any of those games. When I played with them we had to play games they knew, like Old

Maid and Fish. They didn't to want to learn Cribbage, because it had too much arithmetic in it, but I learned all the 15-combinations playing Cribbage. Mama especially liked to play Cribbage with Junior and George. They played so much they kept track of their wins in a composition book. Our cribbage board was special. Daddy made it when he was in the Navy, before he and Mama met. It was made of dark wood, with the design on the top inlaid with lighter wood and sanded so smooth there were no cracks at all. In the light squares he drilled the holes to keep score with little pegs. The board was beautiful. It was then and still is, and it is used daily.

The other thing our whole family loved to do in the long winter evenings (or any other time, for that matter) was to read books. When I was only four, before I went to kindergarten, Thelma and George and Junior were so tired of reading to me that they taught me to read for myself. I was too little to remember much about it, but Mama liked to tell about me coming to her one day with a book to read to her. Mama thought I was pretending to read, so for awhile, just to be polite, she pretended to believe I was really reading. Then she noticed that I was turning the pages and really reading the words. She got out a different book and I could read that one, too. That was how Mama found out that I knew how to read. I had a library card like the rest of the family, and going to the library was one of my very favorite things to do. All those books standing so quietly on the shelves, hiding all sorts of good secrets and surprises inside. They were almost like Christmas presents wrapped in paper and tied with ribbon—who knew what might be inside? I thought it would be fun to start at one end of the library and read my way all around the shelves, one book after another. I decided librarians must be the luckiest people in the world to work in the midst of all those books.

Our library was an imposing building. You wouldn't have guessed by looking at it that it held so much pleasure and so many adventures inside its stolid walls. Square and uncompromising, it rose almost two stories tall above its grassy lawn. The bottom floor was halfway above the lawn and halfway underneath. It was full of reference books and other things that libraries keep in out-of-the-way places. The top floor was the main library where you could go to read and to find books to take home. The top floor was reached by wide stone steps with flat, smooth stone banisters that daring little boys liked to slide down when nobody was looking. I wanted to try sliding, but Mama gave me her "No" look (which was a little frown and a shake of her head), so I couldn't.

Inside the door at a high desk sat the librarian to check books in and check books out, and sometimes to say, "Shhhh" at people who forgot to be quiet. Over to the left was the children's room, with low tables and chairs and lots of children's books scattered around on the tables and in the shelves. Some of the books I read over and over again, even when I knew them by heart, because they delighted me so thoroughly. One was such a favorite that Thelma copied the whole story, writing it out carefully on plain sheets of paper. She traced the pictures on tissue paper and colored them just like the book. Then she punched holes in the edges of the paper and tied the sheets together with yarn to make my very own copy of that wonderful book. That book was all about *Mr. Toodle-oo and the Cockyolly Bird*. I wish I knew whatever happened to that amazing book she made for me, and I wish I could find the real book about Mr. Toodle-oo for my grandchildren, but nobody seems to be acquainted with that gentleman any more. Such a pity.

The most special part of winter was Christmas. First there was the fun of getting presents ready for everybody. At school we were very busy making things—painting pictures, weaving raffia mats, making blotters, and decorating calendars. At home, after Christmas vacation began, Mama took me on my annual Christmas Shopping Trip. I don't know how or when the rest of my family did their shopping, but my shopping was an Event. My Christmas Shopping Trip wasn't at all like regular shopping. Regular shopping was done uptown. Uptown was just a few blocks from where we lived. You could walk there easily, and we did. Often on a summer evening we walked uptown to buy an ice cream cone. Uptown there were the markets that had no real walls or doors on the fronts of the buildings, just folding iron gates that at night the store-keeper pulled across the front and locked together, so you could see in but couldn't get in. There were the good-smelling bakeries and the ice cream parlor and the small movie theater. There was the dark and crowded store where Mama bought my school shoes and the cloth to make my school dresses. Uptown was where we went to shop mostly.

Downtown was different; it was special and important. Downtown was a long way off. You couldn't walk there; you had to go in the car or ride on the street car. I much preferred the street car. Downtown was where the big stores were, and the Bank, and restaurants, and the big Five and Dime. For my Christmas Shopping Trip, we went downtown instead of uptown, and it went like this. First, I wore my good coat instead of my school coat. This year I had a new one; it was dark blue and soft and thick. It was lined with silky material and buttoned up the front with silver buttons with raised designs on them. It was the first coat I ever had that we bought from a store, the first one that Mama didn't have to sew. It would have to last for two years, so the sleeves hung down just a little and it came just a little below my dress—but not too much, because Mama didn't want me to look like I was wearing my "Grandmother's coat." She thought it was misguided economy to buy things so big that by the time they fit you, they were all worn out. With my good coat I carried my purse, a little blue suede one with a strap across the back to put your hand through (very fashionable). When we were finally ready, Mama and I walked uptown to meet my friend Chrystial and her mother at the street car stop.

It was hard for Chrystial and me to stand still and wait patiently, trying to look as grown-up as we could. At last, when we decided it would never get there, the street car came along with a fine clanging of bells. We climbed up the steep steps and dropped our coins in the little box that stood up on one metal leg beside the conductor. I liked to watch through its glass sides as the coin rattled and rolled and fell all the way through to the bottom. Sometimes, though, there were other people trying to get on the street car, too. If there were, I mustn't keep them waiting while I watched. I had to just quickly drop my coin and hurry along the aisle with Mama, listening to the tantalizing roll and clank of my coin behind us.

Chrystial and I were allowed to choose a seat all to ourselves and we settled down on the hard, slick wicker bench, just about suffocated with excitement. One of us could sit by the window going and the other could sit by the window coming back. There was plenty to look at both inside and outside the street car. Inside along the top of the wall, which curved over to meet the ceiling, there were pictures and advertisements about things to buy. Most interesting of all, attached to the wall inside the street car were tall, narrow boxes with a coin slot on top and little handles to pull on the bottom. We eyed them with the greatest of pleasure and anticipation.

On the way home we would each be allowed to take a penny and drop it in the slot. Then we could pull one of the little handles and out would pop a stick of gum. It was an amazing thing, and we would like to have done it over and over, but we could only do it once. And it had to be on the way home—that was our mothers' rule. We were allowed to chew our gum on the way home, but it had to stay in our mouths—we couldn't take it out to look at it or pull it out into a long, elastic string. It was fun just to get it out of the machine, though, and then chew it till the flavor was all gone. Chrystial always took a long time to choose her gum. She looked at each little picture and then chose the same one every time, which was two little squares of white candy-coated gum that came in a darling tiny blue box. That little box was tempting, but I would always choose a long flat stick of gum wrapped first in shiny foil and on the outside in a sleeve of white paper with a tasteful red arrow printed on it. I liked to unwrap it, saving the shiny foil, and fold the flat stick into a little square before I put it in my mouth.

Whenever the street car stopped or started, the conductor clanged the bell loudly. When the car began to move, it started first with a jerk that made us giggle behind our hands, and then smoothed out so we slid along almost as if we were riding on glass. Chrystial and I were too shy to look at the grown-up people who got on the street car, but if there were children, we would all eye each other solemnly. If they looked nice, we smiled at them, but if they behaved badly, Chrystial and I were embarrassed for them and looked away out the windows. Looking out the windows was more fun, anyhow—watching the cars and the houses and stores, and sometimes passing other street cars going the other way. Most exciting of all was riding over the tall trestle that crossed high above the deep canyons near downtown. We would kneel up on the seat (if our mothers weren't watching) and look far down into the canyon. We would carefully watch the long legs of the trestle beneath us, wondering breathlessly if they would break or if our street car would fall off this time. It never did—anyway, not while we were riding on it. When we got close to downtown our mothers would let one of us pull the cord that rang a bell to let the conductor know we wanted to get off. Sometimes, if they didn't tell us soon enough, someone else would pull the cord first. That was always disappointing, but we soon forgot our disappointment in the excitement of climbing down the steep, slippery steps and making our way to the curb amongst cars and taxis and people.

Then came the stores. They were wonderful. We had our favorites. The biggest stores had marvelous window displays of snowmen, carolers, Santa Claus, or elves. All kinds of wonderful scenes were arranged in the big windows. Sometimes the figures moved and then we could have stood for hours watching Santa wave or the skaters skate. At last we would drag ourselves (or be dragged by our mothers) away from the window display. Once inside, we would find our way to the toy department. In the big expensive stores, they didn't just have a pretend Santa Claus for the children to see. They had much more. Sometimes there was a puppet show, sometimes clowns (I didn't like those much). Sometimes there were games to play or miniature towns you could walk through to watch pretend elves making pretend toys. Sometimes there were little slides to go down or mazes to follow with a prize at the end if you figured it out. (One year my wonderful maze prize was a picture book about the darling little Dionne quintuplets.) At the very center of all these beautiful things, Santa Claus, dressed in red velvet and white fur, sat on a big, sparkling throne. Chrystial and I would go up and sit gingerly on his knee, so overcome we could hardly speak, and softly ask for "a new dolly, please." We knew they were pretend Santas, of course. They were really Santa's helpers dressed up in Santa's old suits, but we made sure they knew what we wanted, for we felt they knew Santa personally and would pass the message.

After we had seen all the window displays and the toylands and the Santa's helpers, we studied the Christmas dolls. Our mothers encouraged us in this activity, but I can't say we really needed their encouragement. Dazzled by the visions of loveliness in the doll displays, we would try to make up our minds which one we would ask Santa for this year, while our mothers thoughtfully examined the little price tags dangling from the dimpled doll wrists.

Then with a last covetous look at our special favorites, we would leave the big stores, walk to the Five and Dime, and get down to business. That was the best fun of all, for that was where we could spend the money in our purses. There we would buy presents for our mothers and fathers and our brothers and for my sister (Chrystial didn't have a sister, and she only had one brother). While our mothers waited patiently we agonized over the choice of a handkerchief with blue or with pink flowers, the black or the brown comb, the cunning little round mirror or the coin purse. We bought presents for each other as well, if we could manage to do it when the other wasn't looking. For each other, we usually bought hair ribbons, which involved difficult choices of color and width, and there was much frantic whispering and behind-the-back pointing to enlist our mothers' help in distracting the potential recipient. It was part of the tradition that our mothers bought nothing. When they did their shopping we didn't know, but we vaguely felt that would have to be on their own time—this was OUR Christmas Shopping Trip.

At last, our purses empty, clutching the paper bags containing our treasures, Chrystial and I would be steered to the cafeteria for lunch. Sated with Christmas and Santas and crowds, we would collapse exhausted on the hard, high-backed chairs with our coats hung neatly over the backs. Feet dangling, precious bags under our chairs, we would wait silently for our mothers to bring trays of tomato soup and crackers, milk, and Jell-O. After lunch, and barely able to stay awake, we struggled into our coats, retrieved our packages, and staggered out into the cold (and quite often, a gray, drizzling rain) to wait for the street car. Except for the gum, going back home wasn't nearly as exciting as the trip downtown. Chewing absent-mindedly, we slumped on the hard seats, visions of Christmas splendors whirling in our heads, and hoped we weren't going to throw up this time.

Next (after we got rested up from the shopping) came the wrapping of the presents. Momentous decisions had to be made before they could be wrapped correctly. It was terribly important to choose just the right paper and the right tag. Poinsettias were all right for ladies, we thought, but not for men; reindeer were all right for men, but not very good for ladies; stockings were only for children and didn't seem right for grown-ups. When the wrapping was finally done to our satisfaction, the wrapped presents had to be hidden away carefully so nobody would find them. Sometimes we hid them so well we couldn't even find them ourselves. Long after Christmas a forgotten present might turn up, and usually it was even better for being such a surprise.

When the presents were wrapped up and hidden away, it was time to decorate the house. My family had special and beautiful decorations. Crepe paper and celluloid figured heavily among them, augmented each year by yards of fresh paper chains made by me with much labor and many jars of paste. Trimming the tree was the climax of our decorating frenzy, and the box of tree ornaments was brought out and carefully unpacked. We always held our breath for fear the fragile glass ornaments hadn't survived the year; mostly they had, although there were a few accidents. We had colored glass acorns and pine cones, a glass Santa, and a beautiful glittering glass tree-top ornament with one broken side that we always turned toward the wall. The two ornaments I loved most of all were shaped like tiny clear glass houses, each one with a sparkly bit of tinsel sticking up through the middle of the house to look like a Christmas tree inside.

It was Daddy's job to put the strings of lights on the tree; he left the rest to us. After he had untangled the long cords, he carefully arranged them on the tree with logical and unartistic precision. Mama would study the result carefully and then softly ask him to please change the red bulb here with the blue one there, and put the yellow one over by the star—until he finally stepped back and announced grimly, "That's where they're staying now." Thelma got to put on the tree-top ornament, because it had been bought the year she was born, so it was specially hers. Then the rest of us could put all the other ornaments on, our favorites first, and we finished with the long shiny strands of tinsel icicles. Mama had enough patience to hang each separate strand evenly over the branches one by one, just so. Junior and George wanted to take a handful, stand back and throw it on, but Mama wouldn't let them. At last the tree stood finished, and we could step back and admire it.

While we waited in breathless anticipation (at least I was breathless), Daddy turned out all the lights in the living room and, with a flourish, switched on the tree lights —which almost always responded satisfactorily. I would sit on the floor beside Mama's rocking chair to admire the beautiful sight, and we all sang Christmas carols—all except Daddy. Daddy would lie on the couch and pretend he was tired of all the fuss, but we noticed he stayed right there in the living room, and looked and listened as much as the rest of us. He didn't sing, though. He almost never did, and Mama always laughed at him when he tried.

Then when the presents were hidden and the house looked like Christmas, it was time to make Christmas cookies. Our Christmas cookies were always plain sugar cookies, cut in shapes of trees and Santas and stars and gingerbread men and wreaths. Mama frosted them with colored icing and let me sprinkle colored candies on the top. She spread the cookies out on the dining room table and went around the table frosting them, and I followed after, sprinkling candies with a liberal hand. After the cookies dried so the frosting wasn't sticky, we put them in little boxes that she got each year especially for the cookies. Those boxes were shaped and colored like little snowy houses and had string handles coming out of the roof. They came in flat sheets, and we would spend one whole evening folding and putting them together. We filled the little boxes with cookies, and Mama wrote names on the tags and sent me off to deliver them to people, at least those who lived nearby. Cookies went to the nice lady at the little store on the next corner, the old lady who lived alone in the little house next door, the old man who lived at the end of the street, my Sunday School teacher, the egg lady, the fish man, the mail man—all the people we liked to remember and wish a happy Christmas.

Mama loved Christmas. She loved it more than Daddy did because she knew more about it. When Daddy was a little boy, Santa Claus hadn't been able to visit his family very often. If the children were lucky they might each get an orange and a little piece of Christmas candy, but not every year. It was a hard life for a widow with five little children living on a poor little farm in cold, snowy Illinois with no man to take care of the family. Daddy said they almost always had something to eat every day, but often it was only corn meal mush, and sometimes "not quite enough to go 'round." They were very poor and all worked very hard, even the children; and there was nothing left over for Christmas surprises. That's why Daddy didn't know much about Christmas trees and presents and lights and Christmas dinners and such things. But he let Mama do all the Christmas she wanted. And always, besides other presents under the tree for her, there was a box of chocolates from Santa, because she loved them so.

When Mama was little, her family was poor but not so poor they couldn't celebrate Christmas. One year was pretty bad, for her Papa had hurt his back falling off a roof that he was fixing. He couldn't work, and they had no money and there was nothing for a Christmas dinner, but on Christmas Eve, Santa Claus left a Christmas box outside the door, with some clothes and tea and sugar and a chicken for dinner. The next year Grandpa was better and could do his work, and the oldest boys worked, too, and they always celebrated Christmas just as much as they could, no matter what. After Mama married Daddy and they had their family, she taught him how to have a nice Christmas.

Mama always said you don't need much money for Christmas, just lots of love. Mama and Daddy agreed about not spending much money, but they weren't stingy. On our street lived a man who, as the saying goes, was so stingy he wouldn't throw a bone to a dog. Or to his children. At Christmas time, those children couldn't have their Christmas on the same day the rest of us did, on Jesus' birthday. They had to wait till after Christmas. Then their father would go uptown and take one of the old Christmas trees that hadn't been sold and had been thrown away on the vacant lot. He would take the poor old droopy thing home and stick it in a bucket for their Christmas tree. He and his wife would go to the stores that were having sales and buy toys that were broken or that didn't work. They would bring home those broken things and wrap them up and then call their children in to have Christmas. While the rest of us children in the neighborhood were having fun with our nice new (although maybe homemade) toys, those poor kids would be sitting under their dried-up Christmas tree trying to play with toys that didn't work. It made Mama and Daddy mad.

There was something else that man did that made Daddy even madder. Daddy was walking home from the fire station one day and saw those children sitting out on their front steps. He could smell the good smell of meat cooking inside their house, so he said pleasantly, "I guess you're waiting for your supper, aren't you?" They all grinned and nodded their heads and one said, rubbing his stomach in anticipation, "Yes. Mama is cooking Daddy a steak, and us kids are having gravy-in-the-pan." Daddy was mad all the way home. He got red in the face and clenched his jaw tight when he told Mama about those poor little children having gravy when their father was eating steak. In our house, if there was only one steak it would have been cut into six pieces. We never bothered with steak; one of Mama's good meat loaves was lots better and didn't cost nearly as much. The dinner of those poor little children, though, was immortalized by our family, for it became a family joke. Whenever a quick or skimpy meal had to be served for some reason, we said, "Daddy had the steak, and we're having gravy-in-the-pan."

Santa Claus always came to our house, even when he had so many poor children to visit that he couldn't bring very much for anyone. Once, before I was born, when Thelma and Junior and George were very small, there wasn't very much at all for Christmas one year—even less than usual. The three children had been sick with whooping cough and Mama and Daddy had to use the Christmas money to pay for the doctor and for medicine. Although the children were better, the doctor came one last time on Christmas Eve just at dusk (in those days, the doctor would come to the house when people were sick). Mama was feeling a little sad because they had no money to buy nice things for Christmas, but they had fixed some Christmas anyway. There was a little tree with lights and some decorations, and there were some surprises underneath the tree. The tree and the surprises were set out all ready in the living room because the children were still sick enough to stay in bed in the bedroom, so they couldn't see the tree or the surprises. But the doctor saw them. There was a rag doll Mama had sewed and a cradle Daddy had made. Those were for Thelma. There were wooden blocks Daddy had cut from scraps and sanded smooth, and there were two second-hand scooters, freshly painted. Those were for Junior and George. There were three little stockings with oranges and peppermint sticks. And that was all.

After the doctor went to the bedroom and looked at the children and said they were almost well, he sat down in the living room with the cup of coffee that Mama made for him. He looked at that little tree and the homemade presents, and he looked at Mama rocking in her chair and putting the last stitches in a doll's dress. He set down his empty cup with a sigh, and said slowly, "At home in my fine house I have a big Christmas tree covered with lights and beautiful ornaments. Under it are bicycles and dolls and expensive gifts. And no love." He put on his hat and picked up his bag and walked slowly and sadly down the walk into the dark, away from the warm little house full of love. Through her sudden tears, Mama looked again at their little tree and homemade presents, and she thought they looked very rich indeed.

Sometimes Daddy had to work even on Christmas Day. When that happened our family would wait until he got home to see what Santa Claus had brought. One bright blue Christmas morning I waited on the front steps for Daddy to walk down the street from the fire station. Behind me in the warm house, I knew, my stocking was hanging in the corner of the dining room near the wood stove, and the curtains that separated the dining room from the living room where the Christmas tree stood were drawn together and pinned firmly shut with clothespins, because Santa Claus liked privacy when he worked.

I smiled to myself as I thought about the presents I had hidden under the tree the night before. There was the package for Daddy that Mama had helped me wrap up. It was a new pair of sleeve gaiters. Those were bands of soft, round elastic that men could wear around their shirt sleeves above the elbows to hold them up so their shirt cuffs wouldn't get dirty. Daddy's arms were short and he wore nice white shirts with his uniform, so he liked to wear sleeve gaiters to keep the cuffs clean. I had chosen red ones, because he was a fireman. For Mama there was a tiny blue jug that I picked out myself at the Five and Dime. It wasn't for anything useful—it was just something to look pretty. Mama liked pretty things. To set the blue jug on, there was a little raffia mat that I had made in school. Thelma helped me wrap those up.

There were other wonderful surprises, too and remembering about them I could hardly wait. Keeping all those secrets was a big responsibility and I didn't think I could manage it much longer. There was a marvelous work basket that Thelma had made for Mama. Thelma had let me watch her make it and I never told Mama a single thing, even though I wanted to. To start with, it was a beautiful round tin box with a reindeer on the cover. Inside the box Thelma had glued a lining of cloth with green holly leaves all over. The lining was padded so that Mama could stick her needles and pins into it if she wanted to. Thelma had made a needle book of the holly leaf cloth with little flannel pages inside to stick your needles in to keep them from getting lost. Inside the finished work basket Thelma had put a new box of pins and a little tape measure that would pull out of its little round case and run right back in by itself when you let go of the end. And there was a beautiful new darning egg. A darning egg was a smooth egg-shaped piece of wood on a handle. You would stick it down inside a sock that had a hole in it, and then, holding the sock tightly over the round part of the egg, you could sew the hole neatly together. This darning egg was pink and blue and white all marbled together like an Easter egg. Altogether, it was the most wonderful work basket I had ever seen and I was almost bursting with the secret.

For Daddy, Junior and George had saved their money and bought a TOY! I had never heard of a grownup getting a toy for Christmas, but that is what they bought for him. It was the funniest thing I had ever seen—a silly wind-up automobile made out of tin, with a tin figure of a cowboy sitting on it as if it were a horse. The cowboy had one arm lifted up to his cowboy hat. When the toy was wound up, the car did crazy things. It went forward and backward and around in a circle, and even reared up on its back wheels as if it were a horse. While the car did these things, the cowboy would rise up off his seat and lift up his hat and wave it in the air. I knew Daddy would laugh and laugh at that silly toy (and I was right; he did—for years). I almost couldn't wait for all these surprises, but I had to.

At last here came Daddy smiling down the street, walking so smartly and looking so splendid in his uniform. He took my cold hand in his warm one, and together we walked around the house to the back door. We couldn't go in the front door where the Christmas tree was with all those surprises, because we had to eat breakfast first. I could have my Christmas stocking now, though, while Mama fixed breakfast and Daddy changed clothes. The corner where the stove stood in the dining room had a little clothesline strung across to hang wet socks and things on, and that was where we hung our stockings at Christmas time. My stocking was special. It was big enough to fit a giant and was made of white outing flannel, with a deep red cuff at the top, and jingle bells down the middle all the way to the toe. It had my name embroidered in red letters down the side, with Merry Xmas in white around the red top. There wasn't room enough to embroider Merry Christmas, so it had to be shortened to Merry Xmas, but it meant the same thing.

Mama got my stocking down for me and I sat on the floor by the warm stove to peek inside. There was a sweet little rubber baby doll, and there was a tangerine, and there was a round stick of striped peppermint, and way down in the toe there was a shiny dime. I ate the tangerine for breakfast, with the dolly sitting on the table (just this once, because it was

Christmas). I put the dime away in my little blue purse in my bedroom, so it wouldn't get lost. The peppermint stick I put up on the plate shelf in the dining room to have later with an orange. Mama knew the best way to enjoy an orange and a peppermint stick both at the same time. First you had somebody poke a hole through the skin of the orange—Daddy could do that with his sharp knife. Then you stuck the peppermint stick into the hole, down inside the juicy part of the orange, and you gently squeezed the orange while you sucked and sucked on the peppermint stick. At last the orange juice would come up through the holes in the peppermint stick and taste sweet and sour on your tongue. That was the very nicest way to eat an orange, but you must do it outside, because it could get very messy and sticky. I didn't have time now to eat an orange with my peppermint stick, for it was time to open the curtains and see if Santa Claus had come. I was so excited I could hardly breathe when Daddy slowly took the clothespins off the curtains and slowly, slowly slid the curtains back on their round iron rings.

Santa Claus must have come all right, because the Christmas tree lights were on, and nobody else could have been in there to turn them on because of the clothespins on the curtains! Yes, he most certainly had been there, because there were lots of things around the tree, all shadowy underneath the branches. Best of all, sitting right out in front, was the Christmas doll. Santa Claus always brought me a Christmas doll, not just a little rubber doll like the one in my stocking (which was cute, but was not a REAL doll). The dolls Santa Claus brought were real dolls, dolls to play with, dolls with real clothes to put on and take off, dolls that were given names like real people and who became real friends. Even this year, like all the other years—even though Santa Claus had lots of poor children to bring toys to—there was a Christmas doll under the tree for me. She was a most special, wonderful Christmas surprise doll. There she sat waiting for me—not a new, unknown stranger doll, but my old doll of two Christmases ago. There was my dear old doll friend Shirley, wearing a new wig of beautiful curly yellow hair and a lovely dress of ruffled blue taffeta! That was better than any new unknown doll could possibly be. Mama was happy, too, when I showed her the wonderful surprise. Sitting beside Shirley was Daddy's present, a wooden cradle just her size. Mama's present was a little mattress and pillow and sheet and quilt that she had made for the cradle. What a wonderful Christmas!

For awhile after Christmas there was enough time to play with my new toys and to visit my friends to see their new toys, but pretty soon Christmas vacation was over and it was time to go back to school. I didn't mind. I loved school (except maybe sometimes in the springtime, when out-of-doors needed me in it). In the winter it was nice to go to school and have interesting things to do in your day. Mostly, though, you didn't worry about whether you liked school or not, you just went. You had to. And you had to learn, because that was your job. In our family, education was right up there with Godliness and Cleanliness. Mama's parents were great believers in education. Their boys were encouraged to get all the education they could, and they supported themselves while they did it. Grandma had graduated from a college for teachers, and saw to it that her daughters should do the same, for my ahead-of-their-time grandparents believed that girls should be able to support themselves. So Gladys and Ruth both took teachers' training, although both married before they had a chance to teach.

Daddy had never gone to school beyond the fifth grade, but it wasn't because he didn't want to. He couldn't, because he had to help his mother on the farm. But he never stopped educating himself; he never stopped learning all sorts of things. After Daddy met and married Mama, he encouraged her to help him correct his grammar and spelling. He was a voracious reader and was especially interested in history. He taught himself math and even invented for himself new and different ways of doing arithmetic. He taught us his ways of doing arithmetic, and years later when "new math" was introduced in my children's schools, I found it was just Daddy's math. Daddy and Mama were thoroughly well-educated and wanted all of their children to be college graduates. Unfortunately, not one of us ever graduated from college (although I probably came closest), but it wasn't from lack of encouragement.

School was of greatest importance in our family, and poor grades (if any had had the courage to show their faces) would have been severely dealt with. Knowing that school was our job, and knowing what was expected of us, we all did well as far as we went. Every day when I got home from school, Mama and Daddy would ask what I had learned and I had to show them. Daddy made a blackboard for me and hung it on the dining room wall. He made it from a piece of board that he sanded very smooth and painted many times with black paint, and he added a little shelf for an eraser and the chalk. I was the only child I knew who had her own blackboard at home. On this blackboard each day after school I would write the arithmetic I had learned and spelling words and the history I was learning. Sometimes Mama or Daddy or Thelma or my brothers would think up problems or spelling words or puzzles and write them down for me to do.

I liked the lessons and I liked the school itself. It was a big square building with a downstairs for first, second, and third graders and an upstairs for fourth through sixth graders. Outside the big building was another and smaller building all by itself for kindergarten. I didn't like kindergarten very much. The room was nice enough. There were big low windows, little chairs and tables, and a rough straw mat on the floor that we spent a lot of time sitting on. There were lots of other children, most of whom liked to talk louder or play rougher than I did. I especially admired one little girl, Carol, who had hair exactly like Shirley Temple and wore short, frilly dresses. Carol took dancing lessons, and sometimes the teacher would let Carol dance for the class. I would have liked to dance like that, and after I begged and pleaded, Mama enrolled me in a dancing class for awhile. After one or two lessons the dancing teacher told Mama that maybe I would like some other activity better, so that was the end of my dancing career.

At kindergarten what most of the children liked better than anything else was painting pictures. We had to take turns because there weren't enough easels and brushes for everyone to paint at once. I didn't seem to be much good at painting pictures, although I tried very hard. It was fun wearing the oilcloth apron and standing in front of the big easel, but all my pictures looked the same—a square box of a house with a door and two windows and a crooked chimney. I never could get the chimney to stand up straight, but I kept on trying. I liked to play in the kindergarten "band," which was drums and bells and tambourines which all the children beat or rang or shook while the teacher played the piano. And I liked the games we played and the songs we learned; but most of all I liked to read the books, because they were different from the ones I had at home. When I first chose a book and sat down on the mat to read, the teacher thought I was pretending and when I told her I was reading, she was a little cross with me for telling her a fib. After awhile, though, she figured it out and even brought more interesting books for me to read.

When I was finished with kindergarten and went to classes in the big building, I was asked to read a lot. I liked to read out loud and the other kids liked to listen, so whenever a teacher had to leave her class for awhile she would send for me to come and read stories to her class. Sometimes I even read for classes of children that were older than I was. They didn't seem to mind, and I liked their older books and stories better than the ones in my own class.

School was fun (after I got out of kindergarten) and all the teachers were nice. The only part of school I still didn't like very much was art, because nothing I drew looked like what I was trying to draw. Luckily, we only had art once a week so neither I nor the art teacher suffered too much. I liked all the other lessons. I liked recess, too. At recess time the kids would all run out into the playground to play games. The ball monitors would get the balls and if you could get enough kids together, you could play "kick ball" (like baseball, only with a big ball and no bat). Or you could line up against the wall of the building and play "dodge ball" (which could get pretty rough if the boys played, too). The girls liked to play singing games like "Here Comes A Prince A-Riding," or "London Bridge," or "Go In And Out The Window." We might bring jacks and balls to school and sit on the cement to play, or we could draw hopscotch patterns in the dirt of the playground and hop ourselves dizzy. There were dozens of varieties of hopscotch and sometimes we would try to play one set of each, but we never got finished before the bell rang to send us back inside.

It was fun knowing the children at school, because they were different from the friends I usually played with—the ones on my own block. At school there was Joyce, who was blonde and quiet and shy. She lived too far away for me to walk to her house, but she could come over to play when her mother could bring her in their car. I went to her house sometimes, too. There was Dolly May, who lived near the school, and there was Mary Lou, who took tap-dancing. There were the twins Beverly and Beatrice, who played the accordion and danced. There was quiet little Fern, with almond eyes, and loud, black-eyed Margaret from the

Philippines. There was Lloyd, a thin snaggle-toothed boy, who in spite of his perpetual grin, always looked hungry (the teacher often brought an extra sandwich or an apple for Lloyd). There was Kenneth, with the noisy corduroys, and James, who had red hair and no eyebrows. And George, with smooth blond hair and nice manners.

I walked to school every day. Mama walked with me; I think it had something to do with a bad thing that happened in a canyon near the school, but "us kids" didn't know what it was. Mama and I had a pleasant time walking and talking. It was so pleasant that pretty soon all the kids on the block walked with us, and Mama made jokes about taking her "parade" to school. Going to school in the mornings was nice, walking along in the cool freshness with Mama and my friends. It was much more fun walking and talking with someone than to just poke along all by yourself. Through our alley we went and down the sidewalk to the corner and along the hard-packed dirt path at the edge of the street (where the sidewalk would have been if there were a sidewalk), waving good-bye to Mama as she watched us across the busy street and into the school yard. And the school day started.

Even though I liked school, along toward three o'clock all our eyes seemed to turn toward the big clock on the wall. Each noisy lurch of the hand brought us closer and closer to the final bell that said, "School's out." Then began the rush to the cloakroom to gather coats or sweaters, lunch boxes, books and papers and, if it was rainy, our raincoats and galoshes. In those days, everybody's raincoats and galoshes looked exactly alike. All the raincoats were shiny, sticky yellow rubberized canvas, and all the galoshes were brown. Our mothers wrote our names on our rain things, but still they would all get jumbled in the after-school madness in the cloakroom, and some puzzled child would be left sitting on the floor trying to put on two left-foot galoshes.

Out we'd rush, helter-skelter. There would be Mama waiting across the street to wave us across and ask us how our day had been, to listen to tales of loudly-boasted triumphs (although later perhaps, in the privacy of our own house she might hear some mumbled story of my little failures). Down the street, turn the corner, swinging our empty lunch boxes; down the alley, in the gate, up the back steps. And there we were, at home. It was still there—all of it—waiting for us, warm and comfortable, with cookies and milk on the table and supper in the oven. There were all the rest of the family, busy doing many things here and there, and coming together at last for supper. Around the dining room table we'd sit and eat and talk about our day (bragging a little maybe about what we'd done), and we'd talk about tomorrow (bragging a little about what we were going to do). Having a nice time, safe and warm. All there, all together again. Just like always.

CHAPTER THREE

ALL'S RIGHT WITH THE WORLD

Spring in San Diego is a joyous time of year. The air sparkles. The sky is such a bright blue it makes you squint, and the little puffs of white clouds float like airy marshmallows. The fresh breeze (not cool, not warm) blows little girls' skirts and hair. It blows daffodils in the flower beds, and sets them to dancing like ballerinas in fluffy yellow tutus. It catches the clean clothes drying on the line and blows life into them, like trapeze artists doing tricks. It blows the greening grasses in the vacant lots, bending them all one way in a smooth shimmer like waves of rippling green water.

I was lucky to have vacant lots on both sides of my house. They didn't seem to belong to anybody, or if they did, nobody cared if we played there. The one on the north side was my shortcut to Jackie's house. We worried for awhile when a man built a little house on the front of the lot for his mother to live in. We were afraid she wouldn't want us to use the shortcut any more, but she said she was too old to have flower beds or lawns in her back yard, and she'd rather have little girls instead. So that was all right.

The vacant lot on the south side was full of nothing but grass. In the spring that green grass grew thick and tall, almost up to my waist, and made a wonderful place to play. You could walk out into the tall grass and tramp it down, round and round, to make a little room—all private and hidden from view—a little room just big enough for one or two children, where they could sit and giggle and hide, knowing nobody could see them down in all that grass. There would be nothing but the tall, slender green stems springing up around them and the soft rustling tops bending over them, and over it all nothing but the blue sky and puffy clouds looking down. For a few springtime weeks my friends and I, like industrious mice, would make a whole city of nest-houses, interconnected by halls and tunnels of flattened grass. Sometimes we were allowed to take our lunches out to our grassy nests. We would carry out our little bags with a jelly sandwich, a hard-boiled egg with a little salt wrapped in a piece of wax paper to dip the egg in, and a glass jar of milk with a straw to drink it with. We would eat it all and then lie back in the soft grass and watch the sky and the clouds until we were full of spring.

In that vacant lot there were lilies growing. They were Daddy's lilies, but he didn't like to be reminded about them. One spring Daddy admired some of Uncle Edgar's beautiful pink lilies, so he gave Daddy some of the bulbs to grow in our yard. Daddy planted them and took great care of them and watched them. Every spring, Uncle Edgar would ask if they were blooming, but they never did. Finally, after so many years of taking care of the lilies and worrying about them and getting mad at them, Daddy pulled them up and threw them away. He threw them over the fence into the vacant lot and there those plants lay on the top of the ground. The next spring they bloomed—the most beautiful pink flowers, blooming in the vacant lot with nobody taking care of them. We tried not to mention it to Daddy. Mama wanted to pick the lilies and put them in a vase, but she decided she'd better not, so we just sneaked looks at them through the fence.

Now it was warm enough that the house didn't need to be heated any more with the little stove in the corner of the dining room. It was time to take the stove out of the house and put it away in the garage so Mama would have more space in the dining room. In the springtime Daddy was always in a hurry to take the stove down, just as he always delayed putting it up in the fall until Mama insisted we'd all be sick. That's because, being a fireman, Daddy had a horror of fires and worried that the stove would set the house afire in spite of all his precautions. One spring after a long spell of warm weather Daddy took the stove down earlier than usual. Mama said it was too soon, but Daddy especially wanted to get rid of that stove because it was worn out. After a few years, the body of the stove can get tiny holes in it from the heat, and that can be dangerous. Besides, ashes can fall out of the little holes and make a mess on the floor, and Mama didn't like ashes falling out on the floor. This year Daddy decided that was the end of the old stove. He would throw it away and next winter he would buy a new one. So now that it was warm enough, even though it was early, Daddy got busy and took the old stove down.

It was a hard job to unfasten the stove pipe from the stove without getting black soot and ashes all over the dining room. It was a hard job to take the stove pipe out of the hole in the ceiling. It was even harder to get the old stove outdoors without spilling ashes and soot all through the house. Finally it was done, and Mama could begin cleaning up the mess. Instead of putting it away, Daddy laid the old worn-out stove and stove pipe out in the back yard. "That's the last time this stove is going to make such a problem for me," he laughed, and while we stared wide-eyed to see a grownup acting so silly, he jumped up and down on that worn-out stove and smashed it flat. Then we loaded all the smashed-up pieces in the car and took them to the dump.

The next day a cold spell set in. It rained and rained and got cold and colder. It stayed cold for days and days, so cold we had to wear our sweaters and warm clothes, even in the house. Mama didn't say anything about the stove. She bustled around finding extra blankets for the beds and kept her lips pressed tightly together. Nobody complained; we didn't dare—we were all remembering Daddy jumping up and down on that old stove and taking it to the dump. Then Mama caught a bad cold and was sick. Mama was almost never sick, but she went to bed and coughed all night. The next day Daddy went to town and came back with a brand new stove and stove pipe in the car. He didn't say one word about it. He just got out his tools and put that new stove and stove pipe up, even though it was almost spring and it should be warm. That evening he built a fire in our new stove. It worked just fine and didn't spill ashes all over the floor. Mama got out of bed, and we all sat there getting warm and not saying a thing. Pretty soon Mama began to smile and then she giggled and then we began to laugh. Finally we were all laughing so hard we couldn't stop, and Daddy laughed loudest of all. He never took the stove down too early again.

There were lots of children living in my neighborhood, so there was always someone to play with. In those days and that place, children didn't knock on the door or ring the doorbell when they went to play with their neighborhood friends. A knock on the door was for grownups, and grown-ups were too busy to want to go to the door when it was only a little girl knocking. We had to stand outside the back door and call, "Hoo-hoo! Jackie. Jaaaaackie!" Pretty soon Jackie would come to the window and say, "I'll be out in a minute," or else her mother would come to the door and say, "Jackie can't play now."

Jackie was my best friend, my usual, day-in-day-out playmate. We had the best times together and the best fights, too. Jackie was just my age, but she didn't go to my school, she went to another school instead. Her mother wasn't mar-ried to her father any more and Jackie had a new father. She was the only child I knew who had a step-father. We played mostly at my house, because at hers there wasn't very much to play with—no swing or playhouse or any of the wonderful things I had.

Across the street in a house with big palm trees lived Joann, and she was a good friend until she moved away. Then a new girl came, an interesting and different girl with black hair and brown skin, and she was from the Philippines. We didn't play with Margaret very often, not because she was from the Philippines, but because she was bossy. Down the street lived two boys. One was Arthur. He was a nice, well-behaved little boy and the only child I knew who had a baby, a sweet fat little baby sister. I thought he was awfully lucky to have a baby, and I begged and begged Mama to get us one of those, but she "didn't think so." Arthur was nice, but not very interesting (maybe because he was so very good). Billy was interesting. Billy probably wasn't a very good boy, but it was always fun to play with Billy because he had such exciting ideas. People said that his mother "drank." One day at play we children whispered to each other (as we had heard our parents whisper that morning) that Billy's mother had been heard the night before singing wicked songs, and that shadows on the window blind had shown her dancing on the kitchen table! I often wondered just why it was so terrible to dance on the kitchen table. If truth be told, I thought it might be fun to try it some time. And we children, all of us, would have given our eye teeth to hear a wicked song.

These children lived right on my own street, in my own block. I wasn't allowed to go alone to other streets or other blocks on my street, so these were my usual playmates. Besides the everyday playmates on your block, you would always have other friends—classmates at school, or your mother's friend's child, or other special acquaintances. My favorite school friends were Joyce and Dolly May and Mary Lou. Joyce was quiet, shy, and very blonde. She liked to play croquet and have tea parties. Even when we played tea party Joyce always used her napkin and said "please" and "thank you," but I liked her a lot anyway. She lived in a yellow stucco house that had rounded archways instead of rectangular doorways (which I thought very elegant). We took turns playing at each other's house, because we lived in different neighborhoods and our mothers had to arrange our visits in advance. On the arranged day I would go home from school with Joyce or she would come home with me and we would play till supper-time. Then the mother of the visiting child would drive over to pick her up.

My best school friend was Dolly May. I admired her because she was never shy and never seemed to be afraid of anything, whether it was big dogs or rough boys. In fact, Dolly May was, I suspect now, a tomboy. Her house was on my way home from school and once I got into trouble by making an illegal stopover there on my way home from school. It happened like this. Dolly had a mama cat and baby kittens, and she told me that if I came over she would let me hold one of the kittens. I wasn't supposed to stop anywhere on my way home from school, but I did want awfully much to see those tiny kittens. I thought it would only take a few minutes, but you can guess what happened.

I went to Dolly's house "just for a few minutes," and when I knelt beside that basket with the purring mama cat and all those tiny, warm, fuzzy little kittens, I forgot about everything I was supposed to be doing. Gently, gently we picked up each kitten and cuddled it, holding it up to our cheeks, loving the feel of the little rough tongues and the tiny baby feet with little soft claws. Those shut-eyed darlings were so soft and sweet that it was way more than a few minutes before I finally got to my feet and headed for home. Mama met me halfway there. She had been looking for me all over and was worried and cross. For the first time in my life I got a spanking, and I deserved it. From that time on, I got permission first before I stopped anyplace on my way home from school.

I liked to go to Dolly's house for another reason. I admired Dolly's after-school clothes and coveted them passionately. Dolly's big brothers wore jeans, which were called dungarees in those days. My brothers weren't allowed to wear jeans, because they were considered to be work clothes or farm clothes. My brothers wore knickers or slacks of cotton or corduroy or wool, but Dolly's brothers could wear jeans to play in and even sometimes to school. When they outgrew their jeans, Dolly was allowed to wear them around home to play in. Lucky Dolly! They made wonderful play clothes. A little girl could climb a tree without scraping her bare legs and hang by her knees on the bar without tucking her dress skirt up into her panties.

One day when I was playing at Dolly's big, casual, wildly untidy house, she let me wear an extra pair of her dungarees, and I was thrilled. We didn't have special blouses or shirts to wear with pants; we managed by the simple process of stuffing the skirts of our dresses inside the tops of the pants. I imagine we looked somewhat bunchy, but we were happy. To my immense joy, Dolly let me keep the borrowed pants. Mama was astonished to say the least, when I brought them home, but after a lot of talking and (I'm afraid) whining, I was at last allowed to keep the dungarees and to wear them on very special occasions—after they were thoroughly washed. It was many more years before it was considered really proper for a girl to wear pants.

Another special school friend was named George. He came new to school when I was in the fourth grade and for some reason thought I was pretty much all right. He was an unusually nice, gentlemanly boy. His corduroys were always clean and innocent of patches, his shirts starched and white, his sweaters never baggy like the other boys'. His almost white hair stayed combed, he had wonderful manners, and was probably held up as an example to all the other boys by all the other boys' mamas. It was George who at recess on Valentine's Day sneaked in and set on my desk the biggest and most beautiful Valentine I had ever seen, with a basket and doves and roses and a fat red tissue heart. It was George, too, who brought to my house at Christmas time a beautiful bottle of cologne (the first one I ever had) in a glass bottle shaped like a little old-fashioned girl with a ruffled dress. George came over to my house when he was invited, to play games and croquet. He would have liked to come over more often. I liked to have him come over, but somehow I was glad when he didn't come and I could play with my usual friends. I should have had lots of fun when George came over to play, he was so nice; but sometimes, while we were behaving so proper and grown-up, I would feel like giggling. I couldn't, of course, because then his feelings would be hurt, so we just kept on being dignified and sober. Having George come over to play was different. It was nice and odd at the same time, but he was certainly the nicest boy I ever knew.

Chrystial was another special friend, because our mothers had been friends for a long time. Chrystial's big brother was about the same age as my brothers, but she didn't have a big sister like I did. Chrystial was a year younger than I was, and we didn't go to the same class in school, but we had fun playing anyhow. Once a week our mothers would spend the day together sewing and talking. We would all have lunch together (one week at her house, the next at mine), and then we girls could play together after school. My favorite lunch at their house was waffles with chipped beef gravy. The first time we ate that I was amazed; I didn't know you could have waffles for lunch. And without syrup.

Chrystial had a dog, Pat. Pat was in love with a rock. Pat would carry that rock around in his mouth and lick it and sleep with it. Strange dog. Chrystial's mother made all

Chrystial's clothes like Mama made mine, but Chrystial's mother was so modest that, even in that Shirley Temple short-dress era, she made her little girl's dresses real long. When she tried the new dresses on, Chrystial had to bend over at the waist, and if her mother could see even a little bit of Chrystial's panties, the dress was too short. My dresses weren't as short as Shirley Temple's, but they were a lot shorter than Chrystial's. Mama made my panties to match my dresses, anyhow, so it didn't much matter if they showed a little bit.

Chrystial was especially fond of dressing up and putting on a show. I was a little embarrassed by some of these efforts, but I managed to come up with some acts of my own that I'm sure were show stoppers. Flaunting cast-off finery and crepe paper flowers, tossing our heads and posing like glamour queens, we created plays and dances the like of which were never before seen on earth. Our usual audiences were our mothers and they always seemed appreciative. Once in awhile we'd get together with other neighborhood children and put on a really big show in somebody's garage, complete with announcer and chairs for the audience and blankets pinned up for a stage curtain. Our acts and plays were marvelous, and we felt the nickel we charged for admission was cheap at the price.

Judy was another special friend and I've no idea how our families got acquainted. Judy and her mother and father were "Okies." They had drifted to southern California to try to find work after being displaced by nature and depression from the farm where the father had worked. He found work with the WPA and was pleased and proud to go off to work each morning with his tin lunch pail, like all other self-respecting, self-supporting men. Judy's mother was a worn, tanned and weather-beaten woman who worked like a slave to keep their drafty, ugly little shack of a house spotless. Judy herself was eager for friends and was a good one, too. Young as I was, I knew there was something special about this little family. There was in those good people a solemn dignity, a tense striving to keep their heads above the raging waters of poverty, a ferocious clinging to self respect. And they succeeded.

Judy's mother didn't know much about sewing. Neither did her father. That didn't stop him when Judy wanted a pair of slacks. He designed a pair of slacks for her by making her lie on the floor and drawing around her for a pattern and he sewed them himself. Those were some slacks! Mama "found" several pieces of cloth lying around our house and helped Judy's mother make school dresses for Judy. And Mama saw to it that Judy got a doll with doll clothes for Christmas. After all, we had plenty; we were almost rich for my Daddy had a good job (I was careful not to brag, but I was terribly proud of him).

Now that spring had come, we children could play outdoors after school and all weekend. Outside was nice. Our yard was especially nice. In fact, it was so nice that one year Daddy won a prize (a badminton set) for having the nicest yard in our neighborhood. It was all pretty—front, back, and both sides, but the back was mostly mine. Outside the kitchen door were the smooth cement steps that were so nice to play jacks on. Then the cement walk led to the garage where the Ford was kept. (It was always a Ford, even though we got a newer one now and then.) At the right side of the garage was what we called the Annex. It was a building just like the garage but nicer, with windows in the front and back. It (and the garage, too) had a flat roof with just a little edge all around. One time when Thelma and Junior and George were much younger (but old enough to know better), they stood Daddy's tall ladder up against the Annex wall and climbed up carrying their roller skates. They pretended the roof was a skating rink and had a wonderful time going round and round and doing tricks on that smooth flat roof. Until Mama looked out the kitchen window to see what was going on. That was the last time they skated on *that* skating rink.

Out in the Annex was Daddy's workbench. He kept his workbench and tools almost as neat and clean as Mama's kitchen. He kept some old nails there and a hammer just my size. When he was making something with his own hammer and nails, he would let me pound nails into the thick wooden slab that was the Annex doorstep. He showed me how to hammer them straight, but I couldn't always make them do what I wanted. On his workbench, too, were his shoe repairing tools. When our shoes got holes in the bottom, Daddy knew how to put new soles on them so they would last longer. We usually had two pairs of shoes each—one for play or work, and one for school or best. We only got new ones when our feet got bigger than our shoes, or when Daddy couldn't find any good leather left on the bottom of our old shoes to fasten a new sole on.

Mama's part of the Annex had her electric washing machine in it and later her electric mangle. We may not have had matching dishes or a carpet, but Daddy always made sure Mama had what he called the "right tools" to help her with her work. He was scornful of one of my uncles because my aunt for years had to do her wash in a tub with a washboard. Daddy thought that was a shame. The Annex was a pleasant place to be when Mama was washing or ironing or when Daddy was working with his tools. Sometimes, though, little girls could get underfoot and then it was time to "run out and play."

Just outside the Annex door was one of my favorite toys, my swing. It was a good swing, with a wide seat made of wood that Daddy sanded and painted every year so it wouldn't get splintery. The rope was good, honest, thick twisted hemp rope that was easy to hang onto. It had a nice solid feel in my hands and you could get a good grip on it.

The swing had one tall post as high as the Annex was high, and the cross piece that the rope was fastened to went from the top of the post over to the Annex roof. That made a good long swing. I could swing high, back and forth, chanting to myself the old nursery rhyme about swinging ". . .up in the air and over the wall till I could see so wide, rivers and trees and cattle and all over the countryside . . ." and I could really see over the fence and over the trees and clear over the vacant lot to Jackie's house. If I was sitting on the swing facing the other way, I could see far down and across streets and roofs to just a shimmer of brightness that was the ocean. When I was tired, I could "let the old cat die," which was what happened when you quit pumping and sat very still and let the swing go slower and slower until it stopped all by itself. Or if I was feeling daring, instead of letting the old cat die, I would edge to the front of the seat and loosen my grip on the ropes and take a deep breath. As the swing rushed forward, I would jump off, dizzily airborne for those few wonderful seconds—just like flying.

The whole back and side yards were of hard-packed dirt, rolled nice and smooth with Daddy's big heavy roller and covered with clean white sand from the beach. That made it nice and smooth to go barefoot on in the summer. It was very flat, no rocks sticking out at all. That was because of Junior's broken arm. He broke his arm when he was little—broke the same one twice and very badly. When it was well his arm was still crooked, so Daddy made Junior take a little bucket in that hand and pick up rocks from the yard and carry them away. The weight of the rocks did straighten out his arm some, but it never did get completely straight. The yard didn't have any rocks left, though.

I had other playthings in the yard besides the swing, and Daddy made them all. There was a teeter-totter; you mostly needed two people to play on that. There was a "jumping jack" that Daddy invented. It was made from an old car spring, with one end fastened into the ground with cement so it wouldn't move. The spring curved up from the ground, and on the other end was a wooden seat and a handle to hold onto. You could sit on the seat and bounce up and down until, if you bounced hard enough, you could hit the ground. There was the "go-round," and Daddy invented that, too. He set a heavy post into the ground with the top about waist-high. In the top of the post was the end of a car axle, and fastened to this and radiating out from the post were two long pieces of wood. The whole thing went around and around very easily. You could lean over the end of one of the long boards, lying on your stomach, and push yourself around and around with your toes, whirling faster and faster till you fell off dizzy and laughing. If you were really brave, you could climb up and sit on the ends of the wood rails and get somebody else to push you around.

Next to the Annex was a chicken shed. Chickens are noisy and smelly and dumb. They get sick and get lice and they peck each other. And if you want to have a chicken dinner, what you have to do is not fun. After we gave up on chickens, we used the chicken shed to store things in. Just beyond the shed was my play yard where the big old pepper tree grew, low-branched and inviting. Under its shade in the back corner of the fence was my sandbox where marvelous things were constructed. We built roads, tunnels, and castles (when my playmates were boys) or culinary masterpieces (when my playmates were girls). Beyond my play yard was the side gate that didn't go anywhere except into the vacant lot next door. Almost the best of all my toys was that old pepper tree. It was just right for climbing, and it was great fun to sit up high on its sturdy branches and just look around. Hanging from the branches was a tire and a trapeze to play circus, and there was a rope hanging down to swing on when we played Tarzan-in-the-jungle.

Once when I was playing Tarzan with Billy, I jumped from the top of the shed with a mighty Tarzan yell, grabbing the rope to swing down, just like we always did. This time the worn-out rope broke, and down I went right on my seat, so hard my brains rattled. I blinked hard and tried to stand up, a little surprised to find I was still alive. That's when I found I couldn't breathe. My breath was stuck somewhere under my ribs. I gasped and choked and turned blue while Billy stared round-eyed. "Are you all right?" he asked (stupidly, I thought), but I couldn't answer him. I wanted to run to Mama, but I couldn't straighten up. Bent double and gasping for air I staggered toward the back steps, but Billy finally came alive and got there ahead of me, pounding on the door and screeching. The next thing I knew I was lying on the couch in the living room with a wet washcloth on my head and Mama bending over me, her face as white as the washcloth. I had to rest on the couch all the rest of the afternoon, and it was a long while before Mama let Daddy put up another Tarzan rope in the pepper tree.

Not one of my friends had a playhouse. Daddy made that, too. "Daddy can make anything out of nothing," Mama said, and I believed it. Mama always called Daddy "Daddy" instead of Lewis. I didn't think that was strange, for that's who he was as far as I was concerned. I knew his name was Lewis. Sometimes when we had company, Mama would refer to him as "Lewis," but the name sounded strange on her lips. Daddy seldom called Mama "Ruth." If he was looking for her—if she was out in the yard, for instance, and she had a phone call—he would shout, "Roo-ooth, OH Ruth," but he never called her that. When he came in from work, or if she was feeling bad about something, he would stand and spread his arms wide, and say, "Come here, Dearie." That's what he called her then, "Dearie."

Daddy made my playhouse out of a big wooden packing crate. It stood outside the back door of the house over against the garage. The front wall of the garage was the back wall of the playhouse. It wasn't a pretend house, it was real. It had a peaked roof made of boards with real tarpaper nailed over them so the roof wouldn't leak, even in the rain. It had a real door on hinges that opened and closed, and it had two real glass windows to look out of. The chimney wasn't real, though. It was made out of wood and painted to look like bricks. My house wasn't quite tall enough for a grownup to stand up in, but that was all right. It wasn't supposed to be a grown-up house, it was my own little playhouse.

There were shelves along one wall to keep dishes and things on for tea parties. In these shelves, too, I kept coloring books and crayons, and games, and all kinds of things my friends and I liked to do there. Under one window was a table just the right height and just big enough for two people to color or draw pictures or play a game. To sit on, there were benches, one on each side. They were made like boxes with lids that lifted up, and I could keep things in those benches.

Under the window on the other side was a little tin sink. You could really wash dishes in that sink if you brought in water from the house. When you were through, the water from the sink would run down through a little hole into a bucket underneath the sink and you had to remember to empty it. Beside the front door against the wall were bunk beds for dolls, four bunks built one on top of the other all the way up. Mama made little curtains for the windows and bedding for the bunk beds. That was a wonderful place for me and my friends to play. Boy playmates didn't play there very often, but my girl playmates and I spent hours and hours in that wonderful playhouse. It was the very best, most special thing of mine in the whole yard. Nobody else I knew had a yard like mine with a go-round, or a tall swing, or a playhouse, or a jumping jack, or a pepper tree; and none of those things came from a store. Daddy and Mama could always figure out a way to make things nice without spending money.

The rest of the yard was nice but not quite so special. The side yard past the teeter-totter and go-round was pretty much taken up with Mama's clotheslines, although the lines were lifted out of the way with the clothes props all the time except for Monday. Along the fence and along the house Mama grew pretty flowering plants. I especially liked the plumbago, because I could pick some of the blue blossoms and make necklaces with them. Each blossom was made of lots of little flowers, each on a long blue stem. If you were careful, you could gently pull each flower loose and then poke the fuzzy, sticky end of the stem down into the middle of another little flower and it would stick there. We made long strings of them and wore them for necklaces.

The other kind of flower we could play with was the fuchsia. On the thin green stem was first a round green knob (like a head); then a long, thin pink or white part (like the body), and then the petals flared out like a frilly skirt of pink and white, with lots of little stamens hanging down below the skirt. You would pick one (with permission, of course), leaving a long stem. With your fingernail, you would make a tiny slit in the body part of the flower and stick a short piece of the stem through to make arms. Then you would pick off all the stamens except for two to make the feet, and there was your tiny flower doll in a fluffy dancer's skirt.

Beyond the clotheslines was Mama's lathhouse. It had three sides and a roof and was all open on the front. It was made of laths nailed on the framework in a criss-cross pattern. I liked the patches of sun and shade and the shadow patterns made by the lath. It was a good place to grow plants which didn't like to be out in the sun. There was a table in the lathhouse and benches along each wall, and Mama liked to sit there and do her needlework. Beyond that was the front yard, with a long walk down the middle. I learned to roller skate on that walk with a pillow tied on my bottom with rope because I fell down so much just at first. On one side of the walk was a lawn to lie on and have picnics on and turn somersaults on and try to turn cartwheels on.

Daddy made a fish pond so you could sit and watch the goldfish swimming and see the water lilies blooming. Uncle Edgar had a fish pond at his house, and Mama liked it so much that Daddy made this one for her. Uncle Edgar's pond was kidney-shaped and artistic with stonework around the edges. Daddy's was a marvel of rectangular alignment and mathematical perfection and the cement edges were exactly straight and even. The goldfish and the water lilies didn't mind, though. At one end of the fish pond Daddy built a little arbor and Mama planted a flowering vine to grow over it. The arbor had a bench on each side just big enough for one person to sit on. Jackie and I liked to take our sewing boxes out there and sit in the arbor making doll dresses. Most little girls had sewing boxes and were taught to sew. My box was beautiful. It was made in China of shiny painted wood, and had pictures of strange looking oriental birds on the lid. It was lined inside with pink silk and had a little compartment for a thimble and thread, a pincushion to stick pins in, and a bigger place to keep what you were sewing on. In the lid were elastic bands to hold scissors and a tape measure. I had a little china doll that just fit in my box and I made dozens of dresses for her (with about five stitches in each one).

Opposite the lawn and fish pond the yard was flat dirt now, but when Thelma and Junior and George were little, Daddy had made a vegetable garden there. The ground was so hard he had to make his garden on the top of the ground, in soft dirt inside big wooden frames. He and Mama would pack the children and a picnic lunch into the car and take some boxes and drive out into the "back-country," to where the oak trees grew wild. There were no real forests in the San Diego back-country, and no real mountains. All the land was gentle with rolling hills, big granite boulders, and valleys with manzanita and oak trees. Where the oak trees grew close together, their round, stickery leaves dropped down on the ground for years and years and made thick layers of dark, rich, leafy soil. Daddy called it "leaf mould" and said there was nothing better to grow vegetables in. So while the children ran and climbed trees and boulders, he shoveled leaf mould into the boxes he brought and took it home to make his vegetable garden.

Daddy grew carrots and turnips and radishes and peas and beans. He was very proud of his vegetables and loved to go out and pick a turnip, brush the dirt off, and crunch it with his strong white teeth. When the children were very little (and I wasn't even born yet), Junior loved to follow Daddy about the garden. One day as he followed Daddy around, watching him stoop down and pull out little green plants from the dirt, Junior thought he would help. He went along right behind Daddy, carefully pulling out all the rest of the little green plants that Daddy had left. "I'm helping you, Daddy," he explained proudly, when Daddy turned around and saw the disaster. He couldn't be angry because Junior was so little he didn't know the difference between carrots and weeds; so Daddy just picked up all the poor little baby carrots and beets and planted them again. And they grew.

When we all grew older, that part of the yard didn't need to be a vegetable garden any more. Daddy took up the wooden frames and raked the dirt smooth. He rolled the dirt with a heavy roller to pack it down and raked it and sprinkled it with the hose. He brought a load of sand from the beach to put on it and rolled it again. When it was as smooth and flat as he could make it, he brought out a surprise: a croquet game. While I watched, impatiently hopping from one foot to the other, he pounded a striped stake at each end. Measuring carefully, he pounded the wire wickets in place; and then we were ready to learn how to play. Our whole family had fun with that croquet game. Not one of my friends had their own croquet court and they loved to come over to play with it. Even grownups played and I liked to watch my aunts and uncles play croquet with Mama and Daddy. It was such fun to see grownups bending over the little balls and laughing and teasing and pretending to get mad with each other.

The cement sidewalk that divided the lawn from the croquet court went up to the front door and then on around the north side of the house. Mama grew different kinds of plants on that north side of the house between the house and the sidewalk. That's where she grew the pink and white fuchsias. Calla lilies, too. Once, when I was very small, the Easter bunny left a sweet little turquoise blue Easter egg inside a beautiful white calla lily, nestled beside its long golden tongue. That was a wonderful sight to see. The sidewalk there beside the house had something special made right in the cement. It was my own name and birth date and my very own little hand print that Daddy put there when I was very small. I liked to go and look at it. It's probably still there if anyone looked.

At the other end of the front walk there was a little gate with a hedge growing on each side so that people walking along the street couldn't look right in and see everything we were doing. Beyond the gate the cement steps went steeply down to the level of the street. Our house and yard sat high up on a flat piece of ground and the sidewalk and street were a long way down. When Daddy and Mama first bought the house, the bank between the sidewalk and the yard was just dirt and every time it rained, more of the dirt bank turned into mud and ran down and out onto the sidewalk and down the hill.

Daddy drove out to the back-country again and dug up a lot of smooth round rocks from a stream bed. He used the rocks with cement to build a wall at the edge of the sidewalk to hold the dirt where it belonged. Behind the wall, he leveled out the dirt to make a narrow flat flower bed and Mama planted ice plant in it to grow over the rock wall and hang down and be beautiful. The walls didn't go all the way across the front of the yard; there was room in the middle for the steps going up. So from the sidewalk at the edge of the street you could climb up the cement steps enjoying the pretty terraces of rock and bright purple ice plant until you got to the little gate at the top. And that was our yard.

My friends and I thought we lived on the best street of anybody, because we lived on a hill. Our street and sidewalk sloped down to a canyon at the very end of the street. Jackie lived only two houses away, but her part of the street was much higher than my part, and beyond her house, all the way up to the corner it got even higher. On the other side, Billy's house and then Arthur's house were much lower than mine. This made our sidewalk a wonderful place to play with our roller skates or scooters or trikes or bikes or wagons.

Jackie and I loved to skate, and we were very good at it (I didn't need that pillow tied on my seat for very long). We'd carry our skates out my front gate and down the steps and then we'd sit on the bottom step and put them on. First we'd skate up the hill. If you got yourself all the way to the corner at the top of the hill, you could get going as fast as you wanted (and sometimes a lot faster) by the time you got to the bottom. Only the big boys pushed off hard and came speeding down. Most of us just started out slowly; that got fast enough for us. We would start out from the top, just coasting along gently while the cracks in the sidewalk went click-click, clickety clack under our skates, going faster and faster and faster, until we got to the bottom and stopped in a big swooping circle with our feet turned out to the sides. If we were going too fast, or didn't make a good circle, we sometimes couldn't stop and then we skated right off the end of the sidewalk into the dirt and weeds. That didn't hurt, and sometimes we did it just for fun. Then we would have to skate up to the top again, pushing hard with each foot, our faces getting hot and damp, arms swinging and the skate key on a dirty shoestring around our necks bouncing and banging against our chests. Between times we could sit on our steps in the shade and rest.

Sometimes if we were lucky, the popsicle man would come along, pedaling his special bicycle that had a little square ice box built right on the front. We'd hear his bell ring and rush out with our nickels. He'd open the square lid on top of the ice box, and while the cold came up in a little cloud, we'd decide what to buy. Would it be an Eskimo pie, a colored popsicle, or an ice cream bar on a flat stick? Or maybe my special favorite, a stick of sherbet in a little paper cup to hold it by and when you were all through eating the sherbet, there it was—a cherry in the bottom of the cup.

Jackie was my favorite playmate because she understood pretend. We liked to make up stories and act them out in the playhouse or the pepper tree. Sometimes we'd have our dolls act them out; those dolls had great and wonderful adventures. Together we learned to sew for our "sewing dolls." Sewing dolls were not our regular playing dolls. Sewing dolls were cheap little china dolls from the dime store. Their legs didn't bend, their eyes didn't close, and they didn't have much personality, being generally simply models for our attempts at dressmaking.

We often got out our jacks and balls and sat cross-legged on the cool cement of the porch to play innumerable games of jacks. All of us girls had our own jacks (some even had colored ones) and we had little bags to keep our jacks in and our balls. We each had our own special, favorite balls. The balls had to be little so we could hold the ball and jacks in one hand at the same time; and they had to bounce very well so there was time to pick up the jacks while the ball was in the air. All the girls were very good at playing jacks, but boys never could play that game very well. Boys liked to play marbles and mumblety-peg instead. My friends and I could play all the hardest, fanciest games of jacks—"Upsies," "Downsies," "Round the World." We loved to learn new games of jacks from new girls at school, and I learned a lot of new ones when we drove across the country to Illinois. If we went through our complete repertoire of game variations, it would occupy us for hours.

A jump-rope was a wonderful toy and only cost pennies. In fact, some of the very best jump-ropes were made of ordinary rope with knots on the ends and could be obtained (by asking, of course) from anybody's father's garage. Ordinary rope was a necessity for the long ropes that took two turners, for "store-boughten" jump-ropes weren't long enough. A little jump-rope was a toy you could use all by yourself. There were so many things you could do by yourself with a jump-rope. You could run, skip, hop, "hot pepper;" you could jump with one foot or two. Each game had a special rhyme that went with it. "Down by the river, down by the sea . . ." and all the others. The long ropes were used when three or more girls were playing together. They were especially fun at school. You'd get a girl at each end and start the long rope going evenly—slap, slap, slap. The rest of the girls would line up facing the turning rope and take turns. You'd wait, watching the rope, getting rhythm, and then leap into the middle under the rope, jumping whatever rhyming game you chose. Then when you were breathless, you'd duck out again, trying not to "miss" or touch the rope. We could keep going all during recess, taking turns at swinging the heavy rope. Boys could never jump rope. Sometimes they would try—and fail miserably, to the derisive laughter of the girls.

Spring was kite flying time. I was a good kite flyer because I had lots of patience. My kite was just a regular kite, shaped more or less like a stretched-out diamond with two thin sticks that crossed in the back to keep the four corners out. A string went across the kite in the back from one corner to the other and was pulled tightly enough to put a curve in the kite to catch the wind. You had to be real careful when you tightened that string. If it wasn't tight enough, the kite would be flat and wouldn't fly right. If it was too tight, snap! The stick would break. You made your own kite's tail of narrow strips of rags knotted together to make it long enough. When you got a new kite, you would have to experiment with the length of the tail. Some kites liked a long tail, some liked a shorter tail, and sometimes if the wind blew real hard, you would have to tie on more tail.

When it was a nice spring day with the wind blowing, all the kids in the block would run out to the sidewalk after school with their kites and balls of string. Usually you would have to run a little way with your kite to get it started, and then, with your back to the wind, holding your ball of string with one hand and working the kite string with the other, you could help your kite to ride the wind higher and higher, farther and farther. Pull gently on the string and it would climb, but pull too hard and it might nose-dive and crash. If your kite got into trouble—if the wind died, or it just began to dive for no reason—you would have to quick start pulling in the string, winding it up as fast as you could, keeping the string tight to help your kite. If worse came to worse and it kept on diving, you couldn't be bothered with winding. You would have to pull the string in hand over hand, trying to keep the kite from crashing down on somebody's roof or across a telephone wire. That got exciting and scary. I always (or almost always) could keep my kite from crashing. I liked to get it up real high and just watch it moving around gently way up there in the blue sky, and feel it tugging now and then on the string in my hand. I used two balls of string to get my kite very high. Instead of having my string rolled into a ball, Junior showed me how to wind it on a smooth stick, holding the stick in one hand and quickly winding the string in a figure eight, back and forth, back and forth, first around one end, then the other. That was a much quicker way to wind the string than on a round ball.

I kept the same kite for a long time. It was my favorite. During the winter it lived up on the rafters in the garage and Daddy got it down for me in the spring. One year my favorite kite had an accident. All the kids on the block were flying their kites and Billy got his kite too close to mine. The strings crossed and got tangled and both kites plummeted to the ground. My kite wasn't hurt in the fall, but in the excitement of running to pick up the fallen kites, Billy stepped right through its paper cover. Of course, he didn't mean to and was sorry, but by the time I got to the house with the ruined kite, the tears were running down my cheeks. That was the end of my favorite kite.

Next morning, after I got dressed for school and came out into the dining room for breakfast, there on my chair lay my old kite, my favorite kite. Or was it? After I went glumly to bed the night before, George had patched the torn paper of the kite. He glued plain white butcher's paper over the jagged hole and when it was dry he painted flowers and a smiling sun on the white paper patch with my name in big blue letters. It was a beautiful kite! I could hardly bear to go to school and leave it, but it had to wait until after school. That afternoon it flew better than it ever had before. It was the best.

The only thing I didn't like about spring was that always I got sick. When the flowers and trees and grasses bloomed, and when the spring fog rolled in from the ocean and the mist lay in the hollows, I began to sniffle and sneeze and cough. No matter what remedies Mama gave me it always ended the same way, with me sick in bed with pneumonia. At first it was a little interesting to lie in bed with my grandmother's quilt over me, my favorite doll beside me. It was nice to sit propped up on pillows and be fed beef broth with crackers soaked up in it. It was even interesting to have the doctor come to see me and listen to me breathing and put his cold stethoscope on my back. But it definitely wasn't nice to be hot and sweaty and dizzy, and it wasn't nice to cough and gag. I hated to stay home from school and get behind my class, but when I was the sickest I just didn't even care.

When I started to get better, Mama went to school and got my books and papers so I could work to get caught up, but it wasn't much fun learning things all by yourself. As I got better I could sit up in bed and make scrapbooks (with a towel spread over the precious quilt to protect it from the paste). I could have Mama's button bag, too, to play with when I was getting better. Mama's big button bag was one of my favorite sick-in-bed diversions. It was full of buttons. In those days you never threw away old clothes. You didn't even give them away. You just went on wearing them and mending them until there was nothing left except patches and darns. Then they went into the rag bag, and when she needed them Mama would take the rags out for quilt pieces or rag rugs or cleaning cloths. Before she put the worn-out clothes into the rag bag, though, she always cut off all the buttons and dropped those into her button bag to be used again when they were needed.

The button bag itself was pretty, and ingenious, too. Mama's sister Gladys made it for her when she and Daddy got married. It was a big flat circle of flowered cloth, neatly lined with plain muslin. Around the outside edge of the circle were sewed ten or twelve small white bone rings and through the rings was run a twisted white cord. The cord was long enough so you could spread the cloth out flat when you wanted to look for a button. After you found the right one, you picked up the knot where the two ends of the cord were tied together, and the flat cloth circle magically became a bag, pulling itself right up around the buttons. Then it could be hung up by the cord on the back of Mama's closet door.

By the time I came along, Mama's button bag had been collecting buttons for almost fifteen years and it was a treasure-trove of buttons of every shape, size, color, and material imaginable. You could stir them up and make little heaps of them, or sort them according to colors or sizes, or just spread them out and look closely at each one. I loved to dig my hands into the pile of buttons and pick them up, two handfuls, spilling over and running through my fingers in a waterfall of buttons. And it was fun to scrabble through that bounty of buttons, picking out, one at a time, the treasures that were special to me.

There were lots of the ordinary, workaday buttons, of course—plain white round shirt buttons. Even some of those were pretty, though; they were made of shell, I think, and they caught the light in little shimmers of color here and there on their polished smoothness. But deep in the bag, hiding amongst the rest were special buttons. These were the ones that had been especially chosen for a favorite garment (long since worn out), carefully cut off and used over and over until there weren't enough of the same kind left to be used again. Maybe there were only two left, or even just one; so now they stayed in the button bag, secrets to delight a child's eyes and searching fingers.

It was amazing to me that anyone could dream up all those different buttons. There was a little red turtle, a green leaf, a tiny wooden barrel, a big round button with a sailboat in navy blue, a flower-shaped beaded mosaic one (from Italy, Mama said), silver and brass ones with embossed patterns, and my very favorite, a little round one that looked like clear glass with miniature flowers embedded in it. Mama's button bag is long gone now, but it kept me company through many endless hours of being sick-in-bed.

At last one year the doctor said that in the spring, as soon as I began to sniffle, they must take me right away from the coast. Daddy looked around, and up in the low mountains east of San Diego he found a place where we could rent a little cabin just big enough for Mama and me. From that time on, each spring Mama and I would pack our things and go to live for several weeks in a little cabin in the dry hill air. Daddy and sometimes the boys would come on the weekends to visit. Mama and I got a little lonely and just a little bored living alone in that cabin, but at least I didn't get sick up there. Mama took my school books with us and each day I did all my lessons. We wrote long letters and we took long walks and played lots of games and it was a nice quiet time just for the two of us.

When I was tired of reading and doing lessons, Mama sometimes made paper dolls for me. At home I had a big collection of boughten paper dolls; my friends and I loved to cut them out and play with them. I had Shirley Temple paper dolls, and Sonja Heinie, and Deanna Durbin and lots of others that weren't pictures of real people. I kept my paper dolls and their paper clothes put away neatly between the pages of old magazines, but I didn't take them with me to the cabin. There I had the ones Mama made fresh just for me. I loved the paper dolls she made, even better than my boughten ones. She would draw them on heavy paper—little girls with smiling round faces and short hair, always with one foot daintily pointed. I colored the paper doll with my crayons (both the front and the back) and cut her out. Mama showed me how to make clothes for her. I would lay the doll on a folded sheet of paper so that the fold was right at her shoulders, and then draw the outline of a pretty dress and cut it out. I would cut out a half circle at the neck, and then make a slit right down the back; then I could color the dress. If I was careful, I could slip the dress right over the paper doll's head, turn it gently and there she was, wearing a paper dress with a front AND a back, just like a real dress. That was much nicer than my boughten paper dolls whose dresses were just on the front and were held on precariously with little square paper tabs.

After awhile, usually after Easter, the fogs and the mist down on the coast would go away. The weather would turn warmer and drier, and Mama and I could pack up and come back home again. It was nice to live in the little cabin for awhile and to be alone with Mama, and it was especially nice not to be so sick each spring, but I missed home and all the people and all the things happening at home. I kept up with my schoolwork, so I wasn't behind my class, but it would be nice to go back to school and play with my friends again.

Home always seemed a little strange when we first got there. I thought maybe it was me that was strange, because I had been away. It all looked different somehow, and I had to go around and look at my playhouse and my dolls and the pepper tree and my swing. I had to get acquainted with my house and my family and my friends and my life again. I had to be sure everything was still the same. Everything seemed the same, and that was nice. Especially, it was nice to be at home where we belonged with the whole family busy and running here and there as usual and then coming back together in the evening for supper. Our suppers with six of us noisy around the table were so much nicer than supper with two of us quiet in the little lonely cabin. That first night at home I would lie in my familiar bed in the comfortable dark and feel my home and my room and my family all around me, and it was good.

CHAPTER FOUR
REJOICE AND BE GLAD

I liked everything there was about summer. I liked the early morning sun peeking in the windows to make sharp yellow corners of sunshine on the floor. We could eat breakfast with the tall windows open and the breeze stirring the thin curtains. After the dishes were done, I could skip outside and feel the whole day there waiting for me to use it up almost any way I wanted to. I didn't have to hurry to get ready for school. I didn't even have to decide right away what I was going to do because I had the whole day to do it in. There was so much I could do. I might play by myself or go across the vacant lot to call Jackie, or read or sew or sit in the pepper tree or swing, or anything else I wanted to do, until Mama called me to come in. I liked the slow pace of the day, the scent of the sun-warm lawn at midday, the shadows on drawn blinds in the cool house when we rested on long hot afternoons. I liked the dusky evenings when we could play outside late, and I liked sitting on the porch to watch the stars come out. Bed-time came too soon, and mothers up and down the street stepped out of their front doors to call their tired and dirty offspring home. Voices called in varying degrees of mood and tone (some even whistled). But we all knew that if you didn't pay attention and run right home, your mother would soon start calling you by your first name AND your middle name and you'd better drop everything and skedaddle. If you heard all three of your names being screamed out loud, you were already in trouble and stood in danger of having your britches tanned.

In the summer I didn't have to bother with a lot of clothes, so it was easy to get dressed in the morning. A clean sunsuit and sandals and that was that. I went barefoot sometimes (especially at the beach) but mostly I wore sandals that left my toes free to get plenty of fresh air and sunshine like the rest of me. For play I had special sandals that Daddy made out of my old school shoes that were too small. There was no sense wasting a perfectly good pair of shoes, so when school was over for the summer, Daddy took my old too-short school shoes and cut the toe part right off. With his sharp knife, he cut across the top of the shoe down to the sole and around the toe. He smoothed off the edges, and there was a perfectly good pair of play sandals. It didn't matter if the sole was a little too short, because now my toes could hang over the end. Those sandals were only for play; I couldn't wear them anyplace except at home. To wear other places I had an ordinary pair of sandals that fit like shoes should. For Sunday or parties I had shiny black shoes, useless things with prissy little straps across the ankle (I didn't like those shoes much).

I wasn't allowed to go barefoot anywhere except at home and at the beach, because you never knew what you might step on or in. Daddy liked to tell me about going barefoot on the farm when he was a little boy. He had to go barefoot most of the time (even in the winter) because there wasn't any money for shoes, and when he went to the barn to help clean out the mess that the animals made, he would have to walk in the squishy, smelly mud. Daddy told me how he liked to feel it squish up between his toes, but I thought it sounded awful. I thought he must have been teasing, but I was never quite sure about that.

When Mama was little, her Mama and Papa let their children go barefoot, too, but only in the summer, and they had a rule. The children could never go barefoot to school or church, but starting on the first day of summer they could go barefoot at home. Every summer, Mama's brothers and sisters each tried to be the first one to go barefoot, but they never could. Mama was always the first one up in the morning, even when she was a little girl, and so she was always the first one to run outside barefoot on the first day of summer. They would all get mad at her because she could get up earlier than anyone else. She always could.

Summer was a good time for visiting with family. Mama's Mama and Papa lived in Lemon Grove, right where they had lived when Mama was a little girl. It wasn't very far from where we lived. In Daddy's car, it was just a nice ride—not so long that you began thinking you'd never get there, but long enough to be interesting. When Mama was a little girl, going between San Diego and Lemon Grove was a big trip. Mama liked to tell how the family went to the Fourth of July celebration in San Diego in those days. Early in the morning Grandma would pack a big picnic lunch in a basket and they all rode in the wagon, pulled by their horse. It took a long time to get to the courthouse in San Diego. There they tied their horses and carried the picnic basket to the crowded lawn, to sit on the grass and eat their lunches and listen to the speeches.

Mama was the youngest child in that big family until her little brother Harry was born. Years later, when most of the brothers and sisters were grown up, another baby came along, the last one. That was Adeline and she was only a little older than our Thelma. All her big brothers and sisters thought Adeline was beautiful (she was), and they spoiled her dreadfully; they always did. When Adeline was just a baby, the family planned to go to the Fourth of July picnic, and Grandma wanted a new bonnet for her new baby. "I'll never forget," said Mama, "how she got her pennies together and walked down to the store to buy the material to make Adeline's bonnet." Grandma bought a little piece of white silk for the bonnet and blue silk for the lining. She stayed up late the night before the Fourth, sewing with tiny neat stitches by lamplight. When it was done, it was a beautiful little bonnet, all gathered and smocked, and she laid it aside ready for the next day. But when Grandma got the new bonnet out in the morning light to put on her pretty baby girl, she found that the beautiful bonnet wasn't white and blue, after all. She was horrified to see that in the clear morning light the bonnet was yellow and green. In the dark store and at home by lamplight the yellow had looked like white, and the green had looked like blue. "That was one of the few times," said Mama, "that I ever saw my mother cry. She was so disappointed that her beautiful baby's bonnet was that ugly yellow and green." The baby Adeline wore the bonnet anyway. There was no money to buy another, and nobody but Grandma knew it was supposed to be different. They kept that little bonnet for a long time. I saw it once, the colors faded to an old fragile softness, and I thought about my grandmother sewing the soft silk late at night for her last baby.

One of the many things Mama "never forgot" was the bitter-sweet memory of the long summers she spent away from home. When Grandpa was laid up with his bad back and times were hard, the two youngest children (Ruth and Harry) were sent away in the summer to live with the kindly Schat family who had a large farm outside town. The two children were to help with the chores in return for room and board, along with eggs and milk for the rest of the family in Lemon Grove. The children were well looked after, and they were well out of the way at home, for by that time Grandma had not only her own elderly mother but her grandmother to care for. Both old ladies had come to California in the early 1900's to live near the family, and for some time had lived together next door in the Little House. As they grew older, it fell upon Grandma to take care of them, so she was quite busy enough without her two youngest on her hands. Those long summer days away from home weren't the happiest of times for Ruth. She always, all her life, loved her home (wherever it was) and was never happy away from her home and family.

Those were long, lonely summers for the two children, but the family they stayed with was a good family and a pleasant one. Mama often told me what a good cook Mrs. Schat was and how well they were fed. Except for one thing. The two children, whose chores included collecting the eggs, developed a yearning for hard-boiled eggs, which Mrs. Schat scorned as common. Every day as they collected the eggs, they thought and talked about eating hard-boiled eggs—lots and lots of hard-boiled eggs and salt. One day they hid a dozen of the eggs in the barn under the straw, and later, when the Schat family had gone into town, the children took those eggs into the house and carefully boiled them on the big stove. Hardly waiting for them to cool, Ruth and Harry took the eggs out into the yard and ate every single one. They tasted wonderful, but the children didn't seem to crave hard-boiled eggs for a long time after that.

Another of their chores was taking the milk cows to pasture every morning. One day Ruth, who was something of a tomboy when she was little, got the bright idea of riding one of those cows instead of walking. The cow's back was broad and flat, and she walked along so slowly that it looked easy, but that cow had never been ridden before, and her back was not only broad, it was slippery and bony. It was simply amazing how fast a big cow could run with a little girl bouncing away on her back, trying to find something to hang on to on that slippery expanse. Poor little Harry ran screaming back to the house, certain that his sister was killed, but the only thing to get hurt was her pride.

Lemon Grove, where Grandma and Grandpa lived, was a fine place to live, I thought, because the train track ran right down the middle of their street. Near the train track there was a giant yellow lemon with the name of the town painted on it to show where the train station was. When it was almost time for the train to go through town, Grandpa would take me by the hand and we'd go down the path to the front gate. There we'd stand to watch the train rumble past or maybe even stop with a frightful hiss of steam and squealing wheels. For a long time I was the youngest of all the cousins, so there wasn't anybody for me to play with at Grandma's house. I envied my sister and brothers because they had so many same-age cousins to play with. When we went to Lemon Grove to visit, most of the older cousins didn't want me tagging along. Except for Helen.

Helen was Mama's sister Gladys' girl. She was nice, and she was beautiful, too—almost as nice and as beautiful as my own sister. Helen often found time to play with me. If the cousins played house, Helen let me be the baby. If they played cowboys and Indians, she let me be the little pioneer girl captured by the Indians. One time they all agreed to let me play was when they played fireman. They took one of Grandma's big blankets outside the house, and all stood around it holding the edges. Then they had me jump off the porch roof onto the blanket. That was really fun, I bounced so high. But Grandma saw and told Mama and that was the end of that. I liked it when the cousins were there (especially if they let me play), but it was fun to go to Grandma's house even when they weren't.

Grandma was a little perky bird of a woman. She bustled all over the house, busy doing things. Grandpa was big and tall and slower and quiet and he called Grandma "Nellie." "Now, Nellie," he would say real slow, "now, Nellie," when she bustled too much. Grandpa smoked a pipe. Whenever he wanted to talk to someone, he would take the pipe out of his mouth and put it in the saggy pocket of the sweater he always wore. Then he would forget about it. Pretty soon, Mama or one of the aunts would come sniffing into the room and walk up to Grandpa and begin to slap at his smoldering pocket. "Oh, Papa," they'd scold him, "you're burning your sweater again!" Grandpa had always liked to smoke his pipe. When Mama was a little girl and her big brothers and sisters were still all at home, her brothers were playing ball one day. They stood near the house and tried to see who could throw the ball the farthest, past the barn and out into the orchard. Just as one of the boys gave a gigantic throw, Grandpa stepped out of the barn. That ball whizzed right past his head and hit the pipe he had in his mouth and broke it all to smithereens—it was his best Meerschaum, too. Mama said it was the only time she ever remembered her Papa spanking any of them, but that brother got a good one that time.

Down the street from Grandma's house, before you got to the church, there was a little market, where Grandpa liked to go to visit with his friends. Outside the store was a bench in the sun where the men liked to sit and talk and smoke their pipes. Sometimes Grandpa would go into the store and buy a roll of the spicy rich salami that he loved, although Grandma said it wasn't good for him. If he did eat some while he was at the store visiting and talking, she could smell it on him when he came back and she would scold him soundly. I felt sorry for Grandpa, because I liked salami, too. When Grandma sent me down to the store to tell Grandpa to come home for dinner, he would cut a little slice off his big salami and give it to me. "Eat it up quick," he'd say, his eyes twinkling over the joke, "and don't you tell your Grandma." I did eat it up, and I didn't tell. I think she knew, though.

I did like that store. It was dark and cool inside and there were such tantalizing odors. I liked to watch the butcher sweeping up the sawdust on the floor. They had the best candy in that store. There were little candies with holes in them, strung on elastic so you could put them around your neck and wear them like a necklace. I liked to pull the elastic up and get some of the candies in my mouth to suck while I was wearing the candy necklace. If Mama saw me do that she always jerked it out of my mouth, and then it slapped wet and sticky against my Adam's apple. Another of my favorite kinds of candy was shaped like hard little brown barrels (that was root beer) or red raspberries or yellow lemons. Or there were sugar-covered sticks of hard brown candy that was called horehound, with a dark brown taste that was different from anything else in the world. There were funny soft candies shaped like yellow peanuts, and long black licorice whips and Cracker Jacks with good prizes inside. I liked to look at all the candies before I chose one at last. When I got back to Grandma's house with my candy, Grandma would say, "That junk! It will make you sick!" But it never did.

Grandma had a wonderful pantry in her kitchen. It was like a big closet lined with shelves where she kept her flour and sugar and pickles and things. And her cookie jar. "You must never ask Grandma for cookies," Mama reminded me whenever we started out to visit Grandma, and I never did—I remembered what Mama said. One day while Grandma and Mama and the aunts sat at the kitchen table and had their tea and talked, I stood by the pantry door and looked and looked at that cookie jar on the shelf (I was very little). Finally Grandma asked, "Beverley Jean," (she always used my two names), "what are you looking at?" I said (being very good), "I'm just admiring your cookie jar, Grandma, but I'm not asking for any cookies!" Grandma and the aunts all laughed. Even Mama smiled, although she put on her gentle frown and shook her head at me. "Oh, Ruth," said Grandma, "one cookie won't spoil her!" and she got up to get one for me. I carried it outdoors and sat on the back step, nibbling its crunchy sweetness, and looked at the lemon tree in the backyard.

I remember Grandma and her cookies and her bustling around, but one day when we went to see her everything was different. All the aunts and uncles were there and nobody was joking and talking like they usually were. Grandma was in bed—during the day! Mama took me into the big bedroom to see Grandma and lifted me up beside her on the high bed with the dark carved headboard. Grandma looked different. I had never seen her with her long white hair lying down over her shoulders. It was braided in two pigtails, just like a little girl. I cuddled against her and stroked her pretty braids, and she raised her hand and softly patted my cheek. Mama carried me out of the room and Daddy took me home. Mama didn't come with us then. She stayed, and the aunts and uncles brought her home later. I didn't see Grandma again.

After that, Grandpa lived alone in the Big House until Uncle Edgar and his family moved from the Little House to live with him. The Big House was still the same in a way, but it was different too. My aunt was nice and I loved her, but she was big and capable, not little and perky and bustling. We didn't seem to go to visit in Lemon Grove quite as often as we used to and after awhile Grandpa moved to another city to live with Aunt Adeline and her husband and little Joan. We went there to visit sometimes, so that we could see all of them. Pretty soon Joan had a baby sister and then a little baby brother. It was kind of fun to visit them because all at once and for a change, I was the oldest cousin there. I thought that would made me big and important, but I wasn't used to being the oldest and I don't think I fooled them into thinking I was important. I was still sober and knobby-kneed and Joan was still as adorable as always, so those visits never turned out quite like I hoped. I missed having Grandma and Grandpa where they belonged in the Big House in Lemon Grove.

Those were long trips, the ones we made to visit Aunt Adeline, and I got tired of riding all that way. Mama liked to go, because it was her sister and her Papa. Daddy liked to go because he liked to drive. Daddy always liked to drive, and he was an expert driver. He had only one accident in his whole life, and then he wasn't even in the car. It was like this. When Thelma and Junior and George were very small, the family lived in a house on the edge of a steep little canyon. One day when the family was getting ready to go to see Grandma and Grandpa in Lemon Grove, they packed the car and put the children into the back seat. Then Mama called from the house and Daddy hurried to see what she wanted. Junior was an adventurous toddler and thought driving looked pretty easy and he'd give it a try. He climbed over into the front seat and somehow managed to release the brake. To his surprise, the car began to roll forward down the hill. It rolled slowly at first, then gathered speed, bumping and jolting along. Right over the lip of the canyon it rolled, with the frightened children crying inside.

Mama rushed screaming out of the house and Daddy ran leaping after the moving car, trying to get the door open so he could reach the brake. Down the hill it rolled, clear to the bottom, where it ran smack into the other side of the hill and buried its nose in the dirt. Tearing down the hill as fast as she could go, Mama tripped and fell onto her knees and slid all the rest of the way down to the car. At the bottom, Daddy frantically jerked open the door of the car, and when Mama came up limping and panting, all the crying children were out of the car and in his arms. They didn't have a scratch on them, but Mama's poor knees were skinned and bleeding, and they never did work quite right after that.

When my sister and brothers were very little, the car Daddy had at the time had wooden floor boards and gradually the boards got big cracks between them. That made it very convenient for the little boys if they forgot to "go" before they left home, and if Daddy wouldn't stop for them. Mama was scandalized, but Daddy laughed at the thought of the little wet trail the car was leaving behind it. When there had been a good rain, Daddy would load the car with the three children and then drive through the biggest mud puddles he could find, lickety-split. He'd get going fast and then yell, "Hold your feet up!" and they would hold their feet up and hang on like mad while the car splashed through the puddles and water came gushing up through the cracks between those floorboards.

August was my favorite part of the summer, because that was the month of my birthday. Each year Mama made a party for me and my friends. There were games to play for prizes, and there was cake and sometimes ice cream. We decorated the dining room with crepe paper streamers and we made little candy baskets with mints. Sometimes Mama bought colored paper "poppers" to pull open with a little bang and find party hats and prizes inside. There were even presents for me to unwrap. Before the party Mama reminded me to thank everyone the same, no matter what the present was. I had no trouble doing that; I liked them all. Sometimes it was a book (that's how I was introduced to Louisa May Alcott), sometimes new crayons, once enough cloth for a new dress, and once (this from Judy) a shiny quarter. At my parties everybody who came got a little present from me to take home with them. It was always something that Mama and I had made, like new jacks bags for the girls and new marble bags for the boys. After the party was over and everybody had gone home and we had cleaned up the mess, we would have scrambled eggs for supper, because we were full of cake and ice cream and we were so tired from getting ready and cleaning up after. I didn't care about getting tired, though, because my parties were so good.

My brothers' birthday was only five days after mine, so Mama had lots of birthday celebrations to think about at one time. George and Junior were too big for parties now, so instead they could choose a special treat. One year their choice was a picnic at the beach. Mama made her good chili beans and two apple pies, because that was what the boys wanted instead of cake. Daddy loaded the car with towels and sweaters and blankets and beach balls and dishes and a pot to heat water for tea and everything. We all piled in and Daddy drove down to the beach. While we drove, Mama kept thinking of what we might have forgotten. "Daddy, did you get the towels?" "Yes, Dearie." "Did you get the blankets?" "Yes, Dearie." "Did you get the beans?" "Ye—Uh-oh!" Daddy forgot the beans! We had gone too far to turn back and we still had the potato salad and the apple pies, but Mama wasn't very pleased and Daddy got real quiet.

Daddy liked to drive right down on the beach where the sand was wet and hard by the edge of the water. Sometimes he drove right in the edge of the waves, splashing the water up on one side of the car, while the boys shouted and laughed and Mama held onto the door handle saying, "Now, Daddy, that's enough." Her saying that never did much good, but he never got stuck and almost always found a nice place for the picnic. So this time, he stopped the car and everyone started to get out. There on the wide flat running board of the car, behind the back door, sat the big green kettle of chili beans! It had stayed right there all the time he drove to the beach and down on the sand and through the water and everything. So we had enough to eat after all.

We often took picnics to the beach. Daddy was a good strong swimmer. He and the boys would go splashing out beyond the waves and start swimming straight out. After awhile the boys would swim back again, but Daddy would still be swimming to China. Mama wasn't a very good swimmer because of her knees, but she loved to ride the waves on the surfboard Daddy had made for her. In those days surfboards were made of wood, and hers was heavy and cumbersome. She would lug it out past the waves and then get on and paddle and paddle until she spotted just the right kind of wave. Mama didn't stand up on her surfboard—she just lay on her stomach—but she was very good at catching the waves. She almost never missed a wave and could always ride them clear up onto the sand. Junior and George tried it, but they either couldn't catch the wave or would lose it before they got in to the beach.

I didn't surf and I didn't swim, at least not then. I just waded. I loved standing bravely in one place on the sand and seeing how high the wave would come. Would it come up to my ankles, or to my waist? I loved the feeling of the water sucking back from under my feet and pulling the sand back with it into the ocean, with tiny sand crabs nibbling gently beneath my toes. The waves were mesmerizing. I could watch and watch and watch. Sometimes I watched them so much and got so hypnotized that while I stood there watching, a big one would sneak up on me and break over my head and knock me down. Then there was always Daddy's quick hand grabbing me and setting me right side up again.

Then there was the sand. It was the most enormous sandbox in the world. Mama and I made sand castles with my sand bucket and the little Jell-O molds Grandma gave me. You could pack wet sand in the little tin molds and if you were careful when you turned them upside down, a perfect little fancy shape would drop out onto the sand. Mama showed me how to decorate my castles with turrets and peaks of wet sand dribbled from my hand. Her dribbles were more artistic than mine. Daddy didn't care to make castles. He and the boys built forts and dug tunnels instead. After we had all played in the water and then got dry in the warm sand, Mama spread out a blanket and a tablecloth and we had deviled eggs and cheese sandwiches and cake.

That was the only part Daddy didn't like very much. He said he had eaten enough sand to last him all his life, and why didn't we go home to eat our lunch. The rest of us out-voted him (although I'm not sure any votes counted for much except Mama's). We didn't mind sand and we didn't want to go home so soon. So we ate all the good lunch quickly and carefully, trying to keep all the sand where it be-longed and off the tablecloth, and hoping nobody would kick sand in Daddy's sandwich. Before we could swim again we had to wait awhile after lunch. Sometimes I accidentally went to sleep on the blanket, lulled by the constant waves and the mew of the gulls, and didn't wake up until the sun was low over the edge of the ocean. Then there was only time for one last quick wade in the shallow waves before we packed up our things and trudged sandily back to the car. Those were good days.

Our family did enjoy picnics. Sometimes we went down to Balboa Park and had big family picnics there with all the aunts and uncles and cousins. Everyone would bring lots of food and it was all good. The boy cousins would move tables into a long line and the aunts would cover them with big pic-nic tablecloths and spread out all the dishes of food along the tables. It took awhile just to walk around and look at every-thing and decide what you would take, and wonder if there would be enough for you to have some. Junior and George tried to figure out where would be the best place to stand so they could get a big piece of what they wanted most, but it never worked out that way. We stood around the tables and said grace first, and then Uncle Edgar made us get in line to fill our plates. That worked out pretty good for me, because he liked to put the youngest first and if Joan wasn't there I was at the head of the line. Mama had to help me a little, or I would have had a plate full of cupcakes, one of each color. I didn't mind having her help because she usually knew just what I would like best. There were dozens and dozens of deviled eggs, and bowls of potato salad and macaroni salad and fruit salad and vegetable salad. There was fried chicken and sliced ham. Then came the pies and the cupcakes and Mama's famous orange sponge cake and a bowl of Aunt Dorothy's cinnamon apples. There was always plenty to eat, even for the boys.

Except for the food, though, those picnics weren't very interesting. After we ate, the men would mostly lie down on the grass to rest and talk a little with their hats tipped over their eyes. The ladies would wander around admiring the beautiful flower beds in the park. There wasn't much for us younger ones to do. At a grown-up picnic like this we had to be proper and quiet. If I were good and waited patiently, on the way home we would stop at the beautiful old merry-go-round at the entrance to the park and I could have a ride. The merry-go-round is still there and still as wonderful, and I find I still like best either the black horse with the flaring mane or the white one wearing flowers. It was awful to have to choose between them. I would regretfully stroke the nose of the horse I wasn't going to ride, then climb on the other and wait in breathless anticipation for the carrousel to start. Slowly at first it moved to the wheezy music, my horse going up and down and around and around, while I pretended to be a princess riding proudly in a royal parade.

Our own picnics were more exciting, because our family liked to do things besides eat and nap and go for sedate little walks. A favorite place for our picnics was a wooded canyon with a little stream going through. In those days it was way out in the back-country; now it is buried in a sub-division. Across the creek an enterprising soul had fastened a stout cable from one tree to another and on the cable hung an old automobile tire. You could haul the tire over to your side of the creek by the rope hanging from it, climb up and sit on the tire and push off. If you pushed off hard enough, you would slide over the cable in the tire, clear to the other side of the creek. If you didn't push off hard enough, you would stop in the middle, hanging there over the creek, and have to holler for somebody to pull you back.

Once when we went there for a picnic, Junior and George raced (as usual) to see who could get the tire first. Junior won. He climbed into the tire and gave a giant push. The tire slid along the cable just fine, but in the middle Junior began yelling and waving his arms around frantically. None of us could figure out what was the matter, but finally Daddy got the rope and hauled him back to the bank. Junior jumped out of the tire and rushed behind the bushes, pulling off his clothes and hollering. We thought he had gone crazy till Daddy looked at the cable the tire was hanging on. The cable was covered with big black ants, cleverly walking from one side of the creek to the other. As the tire slid along the cable, the ants were knocked off. They fell on Junior, down his neck and under his clothes, crawling all over him and having their own picnic lunch at his expense.

Another accident that happened at the same picnic spot was Thelma's famous hanging. Daddy had brought a long rope to throw over a high tree branch for the older three to play on. The boys had fun pulling each other up and down, one on each end of the rope over the branch. Thelma wanted to try it, too, but her hands were too weak. She couldn't hang onto the rope long enough for them to lift her, so they knotted the rope around her waist and began hauling her up. The rope slipped up under her arms and as she struggled with it, the rope tightened up. She couldn't breathe, much less yell at her brothers to let her down, and they just thought she was showing off with her wild antics. Daddy finally looked over to see what was going on and there was his oldest daughter turning blue. He got her down in time, but she was madder than a wet hen.

Our picnics were always interesting and much more exciting than the big ones in the park, and in spite of everything, we enjoyed them a lot more. Sometimes we wouldn't make any plans. We'd just get in the car with a picnic lunch in the basket and go for a drive, with no place special in mind. Daddy called that going for a "joy-ride." Mostly we went out in the back-country to see if we could find some different roads for him to explore and some new streams or hills or valleys or other interesting things. When we started getting hungry (which was usually right away), we would begin looking for a good place to have lunch. Daddy wanted a tree. Mama wanted a little stream. The boys wanted rocks to climb on. Thelma wanted grass to sit on. I just wanted to get out of the car. Sometimes it was way past lunch time before we found a place that suited most of us, and sometimes we never did find a good place and would have to park beside the road and sit on the running board to eat our picnic.

When Thelma and Junior and George got older, they didn't like to go joy-riding any more. They would rather have stayed home to do other things. If we stopped to see something interesting, they would sit in the car and sulk and not even look out the windows. That would make Daddy angry and he would pull open the car door and tell them, "I brought you out here to have a good time, and by golly (he never said anything stronger than "golly"), you're going to get out of this car and have a good time whether you like it or not." That usually made them laugh a little. In fact, they got so they could say it right along with Daddy, word for word, and then we would all have to laugh.

Summertime was the time for playing and visiting and picnics. It was also the only time we could make the long trip back East to visit Daddy's folks. They had always lived in Illinois and still lived there, Daddy's mother and three brothers with their families. Daddy was the only one of that family who ever went out West. The rest of them stayed right there, but not him. He loved the sound of a train whistle, for that train was going someplace interesting. And he loved a new road heading for the horizon, for who knew what was at the end of it. Daddy had wanted to see the world and that was why he had joined the Navy. He wanted to be "up and do-ing," not staying right where he was born. He had no pa-tience with "stick-in-the-muds." But even if his family wouldn't budge, he still loved them and wanted to see them whenever he could.

The long trip cost a lot of money, and so sometimes he had to go by himself. One year Mama and Daddy worked hard to save money so our whole family could go back East and meet all Daddy's folks. Thelma didn't go, after all. She was too old for Mama and Daddy to make her go, and they couldn't make her want to. All the rest of us went. Daddy drove the whole way and it was a long ride and took days and days. The car was crowded with five of us in it with our clothes and food to eat and towels and blankets. There were-n't any motels in those days. There were hotels in cities, but we couldn't afford to stay in those. On the edge of towns there were sometimes groups of cabins that were called "Auto Courts" (the forerunner of motels). Most of them had cooking stoves so Mama could fix our supper and our break-fast and make lunches to take with us the next day. She cooked most of our meals because it was too expensive to eat in restaurants every day.

It was at one of those Auto Courts that we almost lost George. It was a newly built Auto Court, and some of the cabins weren't quite ready to use. It was nice and clean and fresh, so that part was nice. Close on one side of it was the highway. On the other side ran the railroad track, and be-yond was a swamp and river, with no other houses any-where around. The little cabins didn't have their own bathrooms or showers, just one for all the cabins. We went, one at a time (Mama and I went two at a time) to take a shower. After that we had supper and played cards awhile on the little table and then we went to bed.

In the middle of the night I woke up with a start. It was very dark outside, but Mama and Daddy were wide awake. George wasn't in his bed. They began to look; we all did. We looked in the car and in the cabin and in the showers. Then Daddy began looking everywhere else, and at last he woke up the manager of the court and told him. The manager looked very worried and mentioned the highway and the railroad track and the swamp and the river, which made Mama turn white and lean against the wall. The manager said he thought we'd better call the sheriff. Daddy looked stern and clenched his jaw and told Mama to go in the cabin and put me back to bed. We turned to go in and for some reason, Mama glanced in the window of the cabin next to ours. It was a new one that had all the furniture in it but wasn't quite ready to use yet. What she saw through the window of that cabin was George, sound asleep on that bed. He had gotten up in the middle of the night and walked in his sleep right over to the next cabin, got in bed, and kept right on sleeping. From that time on, when we were sleeping in a strange place, Daddy pulled some furniture in front of the door or piled cans beside it that would fall over and wake George up. He didn't get lost again.

It took a long time to drive back East. Junior and George took up most of the back seat while they read books and played games and argued. Daddy would get exasperated with them and say crossly, "Don't you boys EVER look out the window? Look around and see the world." He didn't have to tell me. I sat on my little padded box that made me tall enough to see out the windows, and I watched the world roll by. It was a fine sight to see. It changed and kept on changing all the time, all the way back East and home again. Sand dunes and red cliffs and long flat roads as far as you could see. Wheat fields and corn fields and trees. And always telephone lines sagging down, curving up, down, up, until I became hypnotized into a nap from watching them. Then came towns and farms like green patchwork quilts, and at last cities and traffic, and a river like nothing I had ever seen or knew existed. The mighty Mississippi—not just a blue line on a map any more, but a huge, wide, muddy, unbelievable expanse of river. Even on vacation Mama and Daddy believed in education, and I had to learn to spell all the states and their capitals as we traveled through them, and where to find them on the map.

The only part of the trip I didn't like was the big cities. They were big and dirty and noisy. Uncle George, one of Daddy's brothers, lived in St. Louis. He lived in a house that was tall and narrow. It wasn't separate from other houses on the street, like our house was. Its side walls were the side walls of the houses next door and all the houses on that street were crowded together like people standing shoulder to shoulder. There wasn't any front yard, only front steps leading off the gray sidewalk. There was a back yard, but it was only for Aunt Carrie to hang her washing. They did all their living inside the tall, skinny house, and once you got inside it was nice. One thing I thought was very elegant was the strings of beads that hung like a curtain at the doorway of the parlor instead of a door. The dingy sidewalk out in front of the house was where, in the long summer evenings, the children of the neighborhood played their games—"Giant Steps," "Run Sheep Run" and "Red Light Green Light." I liked to join in their games, but I was sorry for them that they didn't have a yard like mine to play in.

The farm I loved. That was where Grandma lived with Daddy's brother Ernest and his family. It was probably a small and rather poor farm, but it seemed to me a rich and wonderful place. There was a barn with stalls for the animals. There was a pig pen with pigs (the baby pigs were adorable). There were chickens and ducks and there were horses and cows. My uncle let me ride on the big horse when he came back from plowing, and it was very different from riding my beautiful merry-go-round friends. This was high and wobbly and alive and exciting. Daddy showed me how to milk the cows, but I couldn't do it very well and it made Uncle Ernie laugh.

Their house was nice. It had a big wide front porch where we all sat in the evening after supper and watched the fireflies and listened to the whip-poor-wills. The most wonderful thing in the parlor was the organ. You pushed the pedals with your feet (just like Mama's sewing machine) and pressed the keys, and beautiful music came out. At least, it was beautiful music if you knew which keys to press. In the evening, after I was put to bed upstairs, I could lie and listen when my cousin played the organ. Outside the kitchen was the back porch, and underneath that porch was the cistern which held the water for the house. To get water, you had to push the pump handle up and down. The water would gush out into the bucket, unless you forgot to put the bucket underneath the spigot. I thought it was interesting to get your water that way. Mama thought it was very old-fashioned and tried not to say much about her own house at home with real water faucets and her electric washing machine and all.

Grandma lived on the farm most of the time with Uncle Ernie and his family. She was supposed to live with the other uncles part of the time, but she didn't like to live in the cities. She liked the farm best. I didn't blame her. The first time I saw my Grandma I was astounded. My other Grandma was small, but this Grandma was even smaller. She was no bigger than me. She helped take care of the house and do the dishes, but mostly she liked to sit in her little rocking chair and sew. She still liked to make quilts, like the beautiful one she had made for me when I was born. One day when we were visiting there, they had a quilting bee. My aunt got out the big quilt stretchers that clamped together the edges of the quilt. A lot of ladies came over and with their needles and white thread began stitching designs all over the quilt. It looked like a lot of work to me, taking all those tiny, neat stitches, but they had a good time, laughing and talking and working. I went outside and played with the kittens and looked at the baby pigs.

There was still another brother of Daddy's that we visited. I liked it there best of all, for Uncle Charles had a daughter that I loved at first sight. Tempe was older than I was, as old as my sister, as old as my cousin Helen, and just as nice. She didn't think little girls were a nuisance. She wasn't too grown-up to play dolls with me and we even played jacks on their wide and shady front porch. She took me to see a brand new moving picture show that everybody was talking about—"Snow White and the Seven Dwarfs." I loved that movie and was absolutely amazed when Tempe told me that all those people and scenes in the movie were only pictures that somebody had drawn. My brothers liked Tempe right away, too (and they didn't always like all their relatives very much). Tempe was fun. She liked to laugh and joke, and Junior and George had a lot of fun laughing and joking with Tempe.

Tempe and her mother and father lived in a different kind of town. It wasn't a big city like Uncle George lived in, nor a farm like Uncle Ernest. It was just a nice town with wide streets and tall white wooden houses set back from the streets in green lawns. The streets were lined with trees that were so big and so old that their branches almost met over the street. Driving down the street was like driving down a shady green tunnel.

We loved Grandma and all Daddy's family very much and liked to see where they lived, but by the time we had met them all and seen lots of interesting sights, we were ready to come back to California. Now we had all that long drive ahead of us again. Daddy planned out a different route for us to come back, so it would be interesting and so that we could see different things—like the Grand Canyon, which was amazing. But we had seen so many amazing things that we were just about amazed to death and all we wanted was our own house and our own beds and our own friends. Daddy hurried a little, and we were awfully glad to get there.

When we finally got home, we began picking up the pieces of summer to finish it up before school started. One evening the telephone rang at suppertime, and Mama got up to answer it. As she listened, she looked shocked and didn't say much except things like, "When?" and "How?" Then she hung up the receiver and rushed into her bedroom. Daddy jumped up and hurried right after her. The rest of us sat at the table, not eating, a little anxious without knowing why. After awhile we finished eating what we could, and Thelma and I cleared the table and did the dishes and we waited. When Daddy finally came back he told us our Grandpa was dead.

In a few days all the aunts and uncles came to visit and there was a funeral. I didn't go, because Mama thought children shouldn't. I thought a lot, though, swinging slowly in my swing or sitting up in the pepper tree and watching the summer finish. I hadn't quite understood about Grandma— I had been too little. She was there, and then she wasn't. But now it was Grandpa, too. Grandpa was dead. That meant he wouldn't sit on the bench outside the store and share salami with me any more. He wouldn't set his sweater on fire with his pipe. He wouldn't smile and scratch his head and say slowly, "Well, now." This was getting very serious. I felt lost and wondered what would happen next. The summer was drawing to a very different close than we had expected.

That night, while I was just quietly dripping tears onto my hot pillow, Mama came and sat on my bed and talked to me. Not about God and Heaven—I already knew about those things. She just told me a story. "I'll never forget . . ." she said. Almost the first thing Grandpa, her Papa, always did when he woke up in the mornings, she said, was to go to the window and look out. He wouldn't be all dressed because he hadn't shaved yet. He would be wearing his trousers and his undershirt with his suspenders hanging down from the waist of his trousers, and his thick, curly white hair would be all rumpled up. He would peer out at the morning and whatever it looked like, he'd say softly, "This is the day which the Lord has made; we will rejoice and be glad in it." Mama told me that she liked to imagine her Papa saying that now, especially since he was with his little Nellie: "... we will rejoice and be glad ..."

CHAPTER FIVE

THE WINDS OF CHANGE

September was synonymous with school. After a long free summer, my friends and I were usually sated with play and looked forward to the freshness and order of school, but it took our mothers awhile to get us civilized again. We had to get cleaned and polished. Our feet had to get used to socks and shoes and our skin had to get used to wearing all those layers of starched and scratchy clothing. We had to have our broken and grimy nails cut. And we needed our shaggy locks trimmed. That meant a trip to the barber, for girls as well as for boys. Barbers could cut ladies' and girls' hair as well as men's hair, for the ladies' short "bobbed" hairdos were all much alike and easy to cut. Those were the days when women had just begun to assert their independence by cutting their long hair. Coils and braids and heavy coronets were passé. Bobbed hair, smoothly shingled up the back, had become the fashion.

When Daddy and Mama were married, her hair was so long she could sit on the ends of her braids. Her hair was so long and heavy that it gave her headaches. It took her hours to wash and dry that lovely hair, and it was a nuisance to comb and arrange, especially for a mother with three little children. So Mama's lovely hair was cut. Daddy hated to see her beautiful hair go, but she didn't mind cutting it, and she found it to be so comfortable and so becoming that she never grew it long again.

Daddy, who could turn his hand to anything, bought a few barbering tools and was soon able to cut everyone's hair except his own. He was good at doing the boys' hair, and he cautiously and carefully trimmed Mama's wavy bob, but Thelma's fine thin hair was a different kettle of fish, especially since she could never sit still and quiet while he was clipping. The last time he ever cut Thelma's hair was when she was about eight years old. After that, Mama took her to the barber so Daddy and Thelma wouldn't kill each other.

It was a complete disaster, that last haircut. Thelma was more fidgety than ever that day. She squirmed and complained and sighed gustily and got hair in her eyes and nose and mouth. She whined and moaned and shrugged her shoulders and turned her head back and forth and sideways as Daddy tried to run the clippers up the back of her never stationary neck. Stepping back to eye the uneven result, he sighed heavily and set to work to even it up. "Hold your head up straight," Daddy barked, "and sit STILL." Thelma cooperated by gazing in turn at floor, ceiling, and all four walls. The result was now too short on the other side, so he took a deep breath and tried again, producing a scalloped hairline that wasn't really what he intended. Daddy began to sweat. Trying to hold his whining daughter's head still with one hand and operate the clippers with the other, Daddy only made things worse. But he was nothing if not tenacious (occasionally referred to as "stubborn"), and he clipped doggedly away until that hair was even all the way around.

When he was through at last, Thelma's hair was cut perfectly even all right, but it was above her ears in the front and shingled halfway up her head in back. The poor child was half bald. Even Daddy was dismayed, and although Thelma might not have been old enough to sit still during a haircut, she was old enough to be rabid about the result. There is still a wonderful snapshot in the old photograph album, taken at a picnic at the beach shortly after the famous haircut. The snapshot shows a furious little girl who has stamped away from her picnicking family and now stands staring glumly out to sea (contemplating patricide). Her chin and stomach are stuck out, her glasses are sliding down her nose, and her outlandish hairdo is preserved for posterity in clear and perfect profile.

For most of us, after haircuts for school, there was the excitement of getting new clothes. No matter how little money there was, Mama always managed something new for school. It was very important to her that we should never wear shabby clothes to school. We could wear (neatly) patched and mended clothes at home, but not at school. Mama "never forgot . . ." one fall when she was a little girl and times were hard, there were no new clothes for school. Little Ruth was hard on her clothes and her one good school dress had a big rip in it. Her big brother Edgar (who was a fine artist) found their Mama crying in the kitchen while she sewed a patch on the front of the little school dress. He felt so sorry for his mother that he took the little patched dress away from her, and with his paints he painted a beautiful spray of flowers over the patch, and added a garland around the collar. Ruth was delighted. Now it was the prettiest dress she had, and she was sure none of the other girls had such a wonderful brother. But when she was grown up, Mama remembered that shameful patch and was determined that none of her own children would ever wear patched clothes to school.

Mama couldn't very well make the boys' pants, so most of the money for school clothes (what there was of it) had to be used for their pants and shirts and our shoes. Little girls' dresses could be made from almost anything by someone as creative as Mama. She could make pretty dresses for me from the full skirts of her own worn-out dresses, and they were just like new ones. One year long before I was born, just after the first World War, it was hard to find any good cloth to make little girls' clothes. If you did find some, you had no money to buy it, and Mama didn't know how she would manage Thelma's school clothes that year. There was a fire in a clothing factory downtown, and Daddy's fire crew helped put out the fire. There he found out that the manager of the store was planning to sell all his damaged cloth very cheaply, and Daddy was able to buy a whole bolt of light blue chambray, the kind of cloth men's work shirts were made from.

Mama was delighted with the cloth. She put her thinking cap on and thought of ways to make those dresses different so Thelma wouldn't have to wear the same blue dress to school every day. Mama made six dresses, and each one was pretty and unusual. One had a fagoted yoke, one had crocheted lace around the collar and cuffs, another was embroidered all down the front with flowers, another was smocked, and so on. The pale blue dresses were perfect for Thelma, with her yellow hair and blue eyes, and no little girl in her class had prettier clothes. Mama was a fine seamstress and had an eye for design. My clothes were always different from all the other little girls, and I liked that.

Our clothes were ready now and school-time was here. It was time to put on my new dress, take my new pencil box with sharp-pointed pencils and fresh erasers, and my new lunch pail, and go back to school with my friends. It was exciting to go to a new room in the old school building, and to have a new teacher to get acquainted with. It was fun to see my school friends again. Before the teacher called roll, we would look around surreptitiously to see if somebody new had moved into the school neighborhood. The desks were shiny and smelt like polish, the blackboard was clean and black, the chalk was long and the erasers new. There was a feel of pleasurable anticipation to the days. Just like always.

Only it wasn't just like always this year. Things were the same but weren't the same. September came, fall came, the days got cooler, and school started as usual, but nothing seemed quite right. In the first place, I was the only one in our family who was going to school. George had graduated from high school in June, Junior (or Lewie, as we had to remember to call him now) had graduated the year before, and Thelma two years before that. Now they were all working at real jobs, not just delivering newspapers. Daddy kept talking to them about college, but none of them wanted to take the time. They were in a big hurry to be grownups. George was thinking about joining the Air Force, and Lewie was driving a truck. Nobody had time to do the things we used to do. Even though my brothers still lived at home, I was lonely.

Thelma didn't live with us any more. She wanted to be a grownup now, and to be one she had to do whatever she liked and do it her way. She didn't live in our house or follow Mama's and Daddy's rules any more. We missed her, and when anybody mentioned her name Mama and Daddy looked worried. When Thelma came over to visit she seldom had time to make doll clothes or play jacks with me. Most often she and Mama just talked or sometimes sewed. If Daddy was at home, she tried to talk nicely, but after awhile they would both get very loud and red and cross. When that happened, Thelma would throw down her embroidery and flounce out of the room. Daddy would slam out to the garage, and Mama would button her lips up tight. I would run outside and climb up in the pepper tree and sit and think. I would think about when everybody was younger and all living at home and playing games and talking nicely and joking and laughing together. I liked it better then. Things were not nearly as much fun now. Nobody wanted to play any more and they all looked anxious and a little sad.

Another difference this fall was that Daddy didn't go to the fire station any more. He had brought home his heavy red fire helmet and his badge, and with a broad smile, announced that he was retired. At first I thought that meant he was too tired to work, but he wasn't tired at all. He was full of energy and worked all day at home making or fixing things. Daddy explained to me that being retired meant that he had done his job well enough and long enough that now he could stay home with us and he would still get paid—a little. He wouldn't have to go to work in the morning, and he wouldn't have to go out any more when the alarm rang in the middle of night. I thought it would be nice to have Daddy home all the time, and it was. I liked to come home from school and find him there drinking coffee with Mama and talking. I liked to follow him around and watch him fixing and building things. He fixed everything that needed fixing and painted everything that wanted painting. When he was through, he would sit in front of the radio, listening to the news. Sometimes Mama would listen too and then they would both look troubled and sober. That fall there seemed to be a lot of things to look troubled and sober about.

October came along and at the end of it, there was Halloween. Halloween was one of my very favorite holidays. It was exciting to be allowed outside after dark, and I loved to pretend there were really ghosts and goblins and witches. I knew they were only pretend, but it was fun to think them up and scare myself with them. Sometimes naughty boys on Halloween liked to go around and do tricks on people, like dumping trash cans over or ringing a doorbell and then running away, but they didn't do really bad things. Sometimes on Halloween night my brothers would rush back into the house breathless and laughing. When that happened, Mama would frown and look disapproving, but Daddy didn't seem to be very worried. If he scolded them, his eyes twinkled while he did it.

Mama could remember a long-ago Halloween (another "I'll never forget . . ." story), when her own brothers were young and how they got into mischief. The boys (now my uncles) thought it would be fun to take a neighbor's out-house apart, board by board, and carry it up on top of his own barn and put it back together again up there. They planned the trick for days, and on Halloween night they did it. How hard they worked and how quiet they had to be, try-ing not to laugh or make any noise with the boards and lad-ders. They took that outhouse all apart, and hauled all the boards up on top of the barn. Working in the dark they somehow managed to get all the pieces put together. It took them hours and it was hard work. When they were all fin-ished, they climbed down from the barn and stood there panting and exhausted to admire their work. Then sud-denly, out of the night behind them, came a deep voice, "Well, boys, you did a fine job. Now let's see you take it apart, bring it down, and put it back where it belongs!" (The owner of the barn had been standing there the whole time silently watching them work—and chuckling to himself a lit-tle.) Now those tired, sheepish boys had to work all the rest of the night putting the outhouse back together. It was hard for me to think of my grown-up, serious uncles being prank-ish boys, but listening to Mama tell that story I could almost believe it.

Daddy didn't know as many stories about when he was little as Mama did. He was too busy working when he was a little boy. He did remember getting scared of ghosts and witches, though. When he was very little, he and his broth-ers often walked across the fields to visit a little old lady who lived in a tiny cabin behind their farm. She told stories to those children, mostly about spooks and witches. She smoked a corncob pipe, and she looked like a witch herself, Daddy said (a friendly witch). Her stories scared those little boys so much that when it was time to go home in the dusk, they were terrified of every shadow and scooted home across the stubble fields, trembling and shivering, as if the goblins were after them.

Halloween for me was different. In those days and where I lived, Halloween meant getting dressed up in a costume and then walking uptown with your friends to the Halloween parade. It wasn't a real parade with bands and floats and decorated automobiles and horses. It was just all the folks in the neighborhood dressed up in costumes and having fun, walking along the sidewalks, meeting each other and trying to guess who was behind each mask. We didn't go "Trick-or-Treating" in those days. We just enjoyed wearing our costumes and being out at night and watching everybody else wearing costumes and being out at night.

It was fun seeing all those people, grownups and children, parading up and down the sidewalks, dressed up in funny or scary costumes. Some were riding bicycles or tricycles, walking on stilts or blowing horns, or doing other funny things. You would walk along, holding your parents' hands (so you wouldn't get lost in the crowd) and when you saw another small person walking along holding onto its parents' hands, you would stop and try to guess who they were. Disguising your voice as well as you could, you would croak, "Happy Halloween! I guess you're Billy? Or are you Frank?" Sometimes even the parents would wear little masks and big hats so you couldn't guess your friend by recognizing the parents. One year Chrystial and I fooled all our friends by exchanging mothers for that night. We walked along in our costumes holding the wrong mother's hand. Nobody could guess who we were, for she was with MY mother and I was with hers. We fooled everybody and it was such fun. We felt smart and superior because we had tricked them all.

Mostly we children dressed as clowns or hobos. Sometimes we would have costumes that our mothers had made for a school play and then that would have to be our Halloween costume. That didn't work very well because our friends had already seen that costume and could easily guess who was inside it. We sometimes wore masks over our faces and that helped, but the masks weren't much fun to wear. They were hot and stuffy and we couldn't see very well through the eye holes or breathe through the tiny holes meant to breathe through. They made our faces itch and then we would have to lift them up on their elastic to scratch, or to wipe our noses if we had colds (which we often did at that time of year). Finally the mask would get pretty soggy and not look nearly as good as it did when we started out. After a few years of that, Mama just put makeup on my face and covered my hair with a hat or a scarf, and that worked much better than those miserable masks.

After we had walked up and down for awhile and seen all the costumes and guessed all our friends, we would stop at the ice cream parlor to rest and have ice cream sodas at "Miss Tillie's." In her ice cream parlor, Miss Tillie had little round tables and fancy white iron chairs with curlicues on the backs. Chrystial liked ice cream cones, but my very favorite treat was a vanilla ice cream soda. It came in a tall glass that was bigger at the top and scalloped like a flower, then narrowed down at the bottom. The ice cream soda came with two straws AND a long spoon. I would sip a little of that tangy sweet milky drink and then dig out a bite of ice cream with the long spoon. When I had spooned the last bite of ice cream out of the bottom and sipped the last sip (trying vainly not to make a "slurp" with the straw), there at the very bottom of the glass was a bright red cherry on a stem. I had to bring the cherry up with the spoon but then I could hold the stem in my fingers to eat the cherry. It took me a long time to do a good job of enjoying an ice cream soda. Usually everybody else was waiting for me by the time I was finished with it, but I didn't care. A good ice cream soda (and I have never found one as good as Miss Tillie's) simply can't be rushed. They are special.

Our school began having a Halloween carnival each year, and that was pretty nice. There was a contest to see who had the best costume, and there were games to play and prizes to win and refreshments. It was fun, but it was crowded and noisy in the school auditorium, and I didn't think it was as nice as the sidewalk parade with ice cream sodas afterward. After the hot, loud carnival, it was a relief to go out into the cool, fresh darkness and walk home with Mama and Daddy.

This year, the year everything began to be different, there was to be a school carnival, and I had a brand new Halloween costume for the first time in years. Mama had made it and it was beautiful. I kept it a secret from all my friends, because I knew they would never guess who I was. I was going to be a gypsy girl. There was a white blouse with red trim and a short full red skirt with black bands around the bottom. There was a little short black bolero with black fringe, and a bright red and black sash to tie around my waist. With it I was to wear a red scarf tied tightly over my hair and (if I promised to be very careful) Mama's long red beads that Cousin John brought her from Italy. There were even earrings for me to wear! Daddy had found some big brass rings and onto the rings Mama had tied loops of thread to slip over my ears, so the rings would dangle underneath to look like I was wearing real earrings. When I tried on all the parts of my new costume, I knew nobody would guess who I was. I was sure I would win the prize for best costume. I could just imagine how it would be to win the first prize—how the principal would call me up on the stage and ask my name and everybody would be so astonished when I told him who I was.

But like everything else that seemed to be going wrong this year, it didn't happen that way. In fact, it didn't happen at all. I got sick, and no amount of weeping or begging on my part would change Mama's and Daddy's minds about letting me go out on Halloween. They did let me dress up in my new gypsy outfit and we lit the candle in my jack-o-lantern, but that wasn't much fun all by myself and I soon gave up trying to make it seem like Halloween. Sadly I took off my beautiful costume and went to bed and read a book, and (I'm afraid) sulked.

I never sulked very long, which was lucky for me, for Mama wouldn't put up with whiners or sulkers. You just better put a smile on your face, even if you didn't feel like it. There was usually so much going on I didn't have time to sulk. Even though Grandma and Grandpa were in Heaven instead of Lemon Grove, the aunts and uncles still visited back and forth. Some of them lived in San Diego or Lemon Grove, and we saw them most. Some lived up the coast in Santa Monica and San Pedro, and we saw them fairly often. Others lived way up in San Francisco, and those we didn't see very much. Uncle Edgar, who still lived in the Big House in Lemon Grove, loved to organize family reunions and then everybody would have to get together. A little girl could sit quiet as a mouse in a corner and listen to all those grown-up brothers and sisters talking and laughing and remembering. Instead of Mama's "I'll never forget . . ." stories, there were *"We'll* never forget . . ." stories, and they told them and laughed and contradicted each other and changed the stories, and had a fine time.

There was always good food around at those reunions, and that made them remember a story about how the brothers tried to cook. They "never forgot . . ." Mama's brothers building a cookstove out of rocks in their orchard and trying to cook potatoes and eggs and things. They did pretty well until they tried to cook a chicken without taking the insides out first. How those grown-up girls did laugh. Then they remembered the "haunted house" in their neighborhood. There was a widow lady who lived alone in an old house. After she died, people could hear terrible moans and groans and cries coming from the deserted house, but when they looked, nothing was there, so they said the old house was haunted. Later the house was torn down, and they found thirty-seven cats living in it. The old lady had loved her pet kitties and after she died, the cats kept on living there and had big families. It was their yowling that made the house seem to be haunted.

Another queer story they told was about Mama and her strange dream when she was a very little girl. She dreamed that she found a big, mean black cat in her room and that she killed it with a butcher knife and buried it in the garden. She kept talking and worrying about it and persisted so long that at last her Papa took her out in the garden to show her it was just a dream. He dug where she pointed, and there was a black cat buried there! Nobody could ever explain that. Another story Aunt Gladys liked to tell was about Mama and her sleepwalking. When Mama was a little girl, she sometimes got up and walked in her sleep (like my brother George did sometimes). One evening, when Gladys came home from a church meeting with her boyfriend (who was later my Uncle Walter), they stopped to talk in the front porch of the house. Standing there, they heard a strange noise on the porch roof over their heads. Hurrying back out onto the path, they looked up and saw a scary sight. There was Gladys' little sister Ruth in her white nightgown, and sound asleep. She was walking back and forth around the balcony in the dark, balanced up on top of the little railing that went around the edge of the roof. They were afraid to make any noise and wake her up, so they rushed inside the house and up the stairs and Walter quietly climbed out on the roof through the window and caught her. They always used to tell her their hair started to turn gray that night!

All of that family took after Grandpa, who had beautiful, wavy white hair. He never got bald (like my Daddy did), but his hair turned white when he was quite young. Just like him, all his children (my aunts and uncles and Mama) had beautiful wavy hair, and their hair turned white very early. They laughed about it and said that they could always pick out their own relatives in a crowd—they just looked for the white heads. They passed on their white hair to their children, as well, and most of us don't mind a bit.

All the relatives got together again when Uncle Edgar's daughter was married. Ruth Dorothy was married in the Big House and it was a pretty wedding. Especially because I was the flower girl. (I think they would have preferred Joan, but she was too little.) I had a new dress of pale green crepe with a dark green ribbon sash. Aunt Dorothy made a little white basket filled with real rose petals for me to carry. My job was to walk slowly down the stairs, past the window seat, down to the parlor and over the path of white satin that was spread out for the bride to walk on. I had to scatter the rose petals across the satin every third step I took. It was very hard to walk slowly and count my steps and scatter the petals (not too many and not too few) so I would come out right at the end. I managed to get it done creditably. I must have done a good job for that marriage lasted more than fifty years. My cousin Helen was the bridesmaid and, as always, she looked beautiful—almost as beautiful as the bride. Daddy never said very much about my cousins, but he thought Helen was pretty much all right. He would say, "That girl has the greatest laugh," and she did and does.

Mama, too, had a new dress for that wedding. That was pretty exciting, for she didn't have many new dresses. It was of silk, a deep rich brown with scattered flowers of orange and gold. She made it with a draped front and a soft, rolled-back collar and a full skirt. When she tried it on for the first time, she came out on our back porch and called Daddy and me to come and look. Mama looked so pretty in that pretty dress. She laughed at our expressions and twirled around like a little girl so we could see the skirt flare out.

Daddy jumped right up the steps and gave her a big bear-hug in spite of all the pins in the dress. Mama would have liked all of us to have weddings like Ruth Dorothy's, with white satin and rose petals and flower girls. None of us did, although I came closest. Not white satin and rose petals, I had a green suit and a white gardenia and an aster-covered arbor in Lewie's garden. It worked, though, the same as Ruth Dorothy's.

There came a day when Thelma didn't come home any more at all, not even to visit. She moved away to another city to live with somebody else, and Mama cried. After awhile, Mama and Daddy and I got into the car and drove a long way, for many hours, to where Thelma was living now. When we found the right street, there she was, waiting in front of her house for us and waving. I was so excited and happy to see her I jumped out of the car to hug her tight. She invited us in, but Daddy wouldn't go in her new house. Thelma got into the car to talk, but—I might have known, the way things were going this fall—everything went wrong.

The three grownups talked and talked and got louder and louder, at least Daddy and Thelma did. Daddy's face got red and then white. He set his jaw and stuck out his chin and banged on the steering wheel. Thelma breathed hard and set her jaw and stuck out her chin and shook her yellow curls. They looked exactly alike. Mama looked from one to the other and tried to say soft soothing little things, but they wouldn't listen to her. After awhile she stopped trying and sat with her chin wobbling and her blue eyes big and shiny with tears. Then that was all and Thelma got out and ran back into her house and slammed the door. Daddy turned the car around and he and Mama and I went back home, none of us saying anything, just looking out of the windows of the car.

George left home to try to be in the Air Force and, although Lewie still lived with us, the house seemed very empty. It didn't matter very much, though, about the house seeming empty, because as it turned out Mama and Daddy and I were going to move, too. San Diego was getting too big for Daddy. Now that he was retired, he wanted to move away to the country. It was too late now to start a farm or a ranch, but he thought he might at least have a big enough place to grow some fruit and vegetables and maybe raise some chickens and rabbits. That part sounded fun, and Daddy and I talked about it together when he lay resting on the couch in the evening with me cuddled up beside him. I thought I'd like a little farm. I'd like to feed the chickens and the rabbits. I wondered where it would be and what school I would go to and what my friends here at home would do without me. I had always lived in this one little house and I couldn't imagine living anywhere else.

Before we moved anyplace to stay, we visited some places just to try. We tried Oregon first, just the three of us. We drove there and rented a wonderful house. It was wonderful because it had an upstairs and a downstairs, and I had always wanted to live in a two-story house. There was a big cherry tree full of cherries in the back yard. I don't know what kind of cherry tree it was, but you could pick off a cherry to eat and the stem and seed would stay hanging there on the tree.

Every day Daddy went driving out into the country with a real estate man, looking for his little farm. And every day Mama had to stay home with me because I got sick just about as soon as we got there. Pretty soon Daddy had to stay home with me too, because I just got sicker and sicker. At last Mama and Daddy decided that Oregon wasn't going to work. The doctor that came to the house to take care of me said we had better get back to California. They packed the car and wrapped me up in blankets and we came back home again to San Diego and the little house that was still waiting for us. I was glad to get back where home had always been. We didn't stay, though.

Between listening to the news on the radio and reading the newspapers, Daddy studied maps. He decided we'd better not go so far away as Oregon, and so he looked around and thought we might like San Bernardino. It wasn't nearly as damp and cool there as it was in Oregon and not even as damp as it was in San Diego. It was warm and sunny there and they thought I might not be sick, as I was most all the time now. We drove to see and looked around and liked it pretty well, so we rented a house to try it out. Then we came back home and packed all over again. This time we left for good. It was just the three of us. Lewie didn't want to come. He had a job in San Diego and a girl friend. George, who couldn't join the Air Force after all, was working and living in another town. Thelma wanted to live where she wanted to live, and that wasn't with us. We packed all our things, and we said good-bye to our house and to our friends and to the aunts and uncles in Lemon Grove, and drove away to the new place.

Daddy always preferred new places, but Mama and I never got finished missing San Diego. After we got acquainted with San Bernardino, though, we found it was very nice there, although very different. What I noticed first of all was the light. Back home in San Diego, the light was so clear and thin and fine that it just sparkled. In San Bernardino, the light was softer and thicker, and somehow not so bright. The next very different thing was mountains. For the first time I lived where I could see mountains, high mountains, sometimes with snow on them. I liked that. They were always there but always changing, and you were always looking up at them. Somehow your eyes are drawn up to mountains, I have found, like running water, or waves at the beach, or a log fire. You just have to look at them. "I will lift up my eyes to the hills. . ." Mama would often say, loving the outline of the mountains against the sky, just as I did.

Another thing that was different here was earthquakes. In San Diego we hadn't felt earthquakes, but here we were living on shaky ground. The first one about scared us to death, and we didn't know what to do. We soon got used to them and would just remark to each other, "Here's another one." Once in awhile Daddy would spot a new crack in the driveway, but that's about all they ever did except to give a little excitement to our day.

There were plenty of things different inside our family. George couldn't get in the Air Force because of his asthma, so he got a job and got married instead. Pretty soon, he and his wife were bringing their little baby to visit us, and it was nice to have a sweet little niece. Mama adored the baby and she and Daddy were quite polite to Alice (I guess being polite isn't exactly the same as being friendly). I thought she was pretty and glamorous. She let me use some of her perfume and she fixed my hair a new way. I liked Alice, but I guess it was just as well nobody got really friendly, for she didn't stay part of our family for very long. She got tired of being George's wife after a couple of years. As it turned out, that was all right, for later he met a really nice lady, Marty, and tried again, and that time it worked very well.

I don't think Lewie thought much of George's first wife, either. Lewie did quite a bit better. The first time he brought Edith to meet us, she rushed in and kissed me and hugged Mama and said "Hi, Pop" to Daddy. We didn't know what Daddy would think of that, but we couldn't help laughing at the surprised expression on his face. Later he told Mama that he liked a girl with spunk. So that was all right.

That was about all that was all right. Almost everything else was wrong. I started to school there, but that's all I did about school. Before I had a chance to make friends or learn anything there at all, I was sick again. It's awful to be sick in a strange town, without any friends to visit you, with everything new and different, and things happening around you on a grown-up level. It was lonely. I tried to get well but that wasn't easy. I just stayed sick, and I got very tired of it. Another thing that bothered us was our house. We liked the house we were living in, but we were only renting it and we wanted a real place of our own. We wanted a home again instead of a house. We wanted to unpack everything and hang up pictures and plant things and you can't do that if you are just renting and are going to move soon to someplace else. So Daddy went looking for our home while Mama took care of me.

Daddy found a house he liked. It was a good house and had a nice big yard. Mama liked it too, and so did I. So Daddy bought the house and we packed again and moved, only this time we didn't have to move very far. We were so happy to have a real place to live that it didn't take us long to unpack. It was a friendly house and it felt like home, almost as much as the one we left in San Diego. This one was white instead of brown. It had a big shady front porch with roses growing over it. There was a nice living room with a lot of windows, which Mama liked, and there was a little gas heater to make the house warm, which Daddy liked (instead of a wood stove like we had before). I had a light and airy bedroom with two windows and so did Mama and Daddy. The kitchen was big and Mama at last had her window over the sink. There was another window too, a big one over the kitchen table, which Mama said was a "breakfast nook." The breakfast nook was exactly like the one in my old playhouse in San Diego, only this one was grown-up size. I didn't have a playhouse now, of course. We couldn't move my old one and the new house didn't have one, and I didn't feel well enough to play in it (even if I had any little girls around to play with me).

There was a green lawn in front of the house and in back, too. Daddy made a big cement porch at the back of the house and built a roof over it to make a nice place for us to sit when I felt like being outdoors. Before we were there very long, Daddy dug up a big flower bed in the back yard for Mama to plant a rose garden. She had always wanted to have a nice rose garden and she had a wonderful time picking out the special ones she wanted. Later, when they bloomed, she would go out in the early morning and bring back a lovely partly-opened bud, still covered with dew and smelling like all outdoors, and put it in a little vase by my chair. It brought the outdoors inside, even when I couldn't go out.

Daddy had a vegetable garden now, and he made a chicken house and raised chickens. I found that I didn't think much of chickens, after all. They were messy and noisy and they flapped and pecked. The rabbits were pretty, though. Funny thing—we sometimes ate fried rabbit or fried chicken for dinner. When I asked, Daddy said that he bought those from the butcher and that when our own rabbits and chickens got big enough, he took them out to a farm outside of town, where they had plenty of room to live happily. So the fried rabbit and fried chicken tasted very good and I didn't mind eating them because they weren't the ones I had fed and patted and named.

We didn't bring our old furniture with us when we moved. It was old and almost worn out. Besides, it would have cost too much to have a moving van to carry everything. All the rest of our things we had brought in Daddy's little trailer pulled behind the car. So now we had to buy some new furniture. First we bought beds and dressers. Then we had to stop. The new house had cost more than Daddy planned for, and there were so many doctor bills for me that Daddy said we couldn't spend any more for furniture. We had to keep the rest in the bank. Daddy never bought anything that he couldn't pay for. He said that was the "road to ruin." When he went to buy a house or a car or anything else, he had every bit of the money in his leather purse. He never used all the money in the bank; he always left some there "for a rainy day." Mama thought not having any furniture in the living room was a rainy day, but Daddy didn't mind sitting on chairs that came from the junk yard or the Goodwill Store.

One day when I was helping Mama dust in the living room, she began thinking about leaving her home town and leaving her friends and her family, and about not having any furniture in the new living room and her chin began to wobble and the tears began to fall. It worried me, because I seldom saw Mama cry about anything except Thelma. So I hurried out to see what Daddy could do about it. He was painting the chicken house, but he stopped to look at me while I talked. Daddy always stopped doing what he was doing and looked at people who were talking to him, even if they were little. He carefully laid down his paint brush on the can of paint, which was strange, for he never put a wet brush down without cleaning it first, and never left a can of paint open. He stood up and set his jaw firm and strode to the house. I wasn't sure what was going to happen, so I lagged behind a little. When I peeked into the living room there was a familiar sight. A wonderful sight. There stood Mama almost hidden inside a bear hug while Daddy wiped her cheeks with his big handkerchief. "Dearie, Dearie," he said softly. We went to town—first to the bank and then to the furniture store, and we bought the furniture that Mama carefully picked out. For the first time we had furniture that all matched: a couch and a chair and something called a coffee table and a lamp table. It was good solid oak, and Daddy approved of that. It was pretty, and Mama approved of that. Daddy found some odd jobs that he could do for a man who built apartment buildings, so he could put his "rainy day" money back in the bank.

Along the driveway of our new house was a long row of tall pine trees. I had never lived with trees before except for our old pepper tree in San Diego, and I found that trees make wonderful companions. They were beautiful to look at, and they made shade to sit under, and when the wind blew (as it did there very often) those pine trees made wonderful music. When the wind blew I loved to bundle up and go out and stand and listen to the trees and watch them fight the wind. I couldn't do that very often, for I was still not getting well. The doctors all said we had to be patient and that I had to get lots of rest and take the medicine that made me throw up. It was hard to be patient and finally Mama and Daddy decided to take me to a big city to see a specialist. I loved that idea, because it was the city where Thelma lived with her husband, and we stayed with her. Everybody was polite and kind to each other again, and I loved that, too. I didn't love all the tests at the doctor's office, and I was disgusted when after all that time and trouble the specialist only said what my other doctor did: be patient and get lots of rest.

I felt happier, though, while we were visiting Thelma. Van, her husband, was a painter (not an artist painter like Uncle Edgar, but a house painter). While he painted houses, Thelma was the manager of the big apartment house where they lived. She had to go shopping one day to buy new dishes for one of the apartments, and I helped her pick them out, which was very exciting. Except for the tests, we were having a pretty nice time until one day when we got back early from the doctor's office, we went into her apartment and we found Thelma sitting on the couch crying over her embroidery. We had to pretend we didn't notice, at least Daddy and I did, but Mama went out into the kitchen with Thelma and stayed for a long time. When she came out, Thelma was all wiped up and starting to fix supper, humming a tune in the husky voice I loved. Mama's lips were tight shut in a straight line, and she wouldn't tell Daddy what she and Thelma talked about until we were home again, because she didn't want him to get mad in Thelma's house.

By the time we got back to our new home in San Bernardino, we knew I couldn't go back to school. I hated that. Mama and Daddy tried to be tactful, but I'm afraid I spent a lot of time crying at first. Soon they found a school teacher who taught only children who couldn't go to school. She came every day to our house to give me lessons, and I found I hadn't gotten so very far behind after all. It wasn't like going to school, of course, but in lots of ways it was very good. I liked my teacher, and I met her other students. Sometimes she would give little parties for all of us. We grew to be friends, although we couldn't go outside and play or go to a real school. There was a girl who had polio and wore an iron brace, and a girl who had epilepsy, and one who had something wrong with her glands so that she couldn't stop growing. Although we couldn't get together very often, we became friends and talked on the telephone and helped each other with schoolwork, almost like real school.

Whenever Mama went to the neighborhood stores she watched for girls my age. She found some, and they soon began coming over to play with me. We had to play quiet things, but that seemed to be all right with them. We liked to play dolls. Even Katy, who was older than the others, liked to play with my dolls because they had so many beautiful clothes that Mama had made. We liked to color in coloring books and play paper dolls and sew. We liked to listen to popular songs on the radio and learn all the words to sing together. We had a good time, but sometimes I thought of my friends in San Diego, and the picnics at the park or the beach, and climbing my pepper tree, and playing kickball at school.

My old friends in San Diego came to visit sometimes. Jackie's mother brought her to visit once; Joyce, too. Judy and her mother came up on the bus, although we knew she couldn't really afford the money. Chrystial came to visit me and stayed friends with me (in fact, for fifty years she stayed friends). I enjoyed their visits, but it wasn't the same. There was too much difference; there were too many changes. We wrote letters to each other for awhile, but except for Chrystial, we gradually lost track of each other in all the changes.

Those changes seemed to be rushing at us with breakneck speed now. Newspapers and the news broadcasts on the radio were sober and apprehensive. "War" was the terrible word that was spoken in low tones by everyone. Winter was on the way, and as the days drew down, the grim possibility of war lurked in the darkness closing in. In those dark, chilly, gray days, it was good to be settled in our new home. I felt safe behind its solid walls, and protected by the row of sturdy pine trees from the winds beginning to rage around us.

CHAPTER SIX

THERE IS A SEASON

Winter came along again, as it has a habit of doing. After so many winters, all so much alike, things were now so changed that it was hard to know what in the world to expect next. Winter in an inland valley near the mountains was a different kettle of fish from winter in San Diego's mild coastal climate. Here it was exhilarating to step outside on a clear blue winter morning, your hands in your pockets and your sweater shrugged up around your cringing ears. The crisp cold air was like a tonic. You could breathe it in deeply, all the while looking around at the vivid rim of the mountains, and feel waked up and ready for anything. Almost anything. I can't say most people were ready that dreadful day in early December when the Pearl Harbor attack shocked the country and the newspaper headlines went wild. Anticipated perhaps, but dreadful news—WAR. After the first dismay and horror, the structure of our personal lives didn't change very much for awhile. Or, if it did, I didn't notice; there had already been so many changes. We were sober and worried of course, and now all three of us listened to the news on the radio and studied the maps. But for the moment, my life at least was more affected by differences closer at hand.

Here we were in a different town, in a different house, no brothers or sister around to keep things lively, only Mama and Daddy and me. No school, no playing outdoors, no familiar friends to keep me cheerful, just having to stay quiet and rest all the time. It was hard to get used to these things all at once, and I wasn't much good to anybody, including myself. Mama found some girls to be friends with me, and I was smart enough to be grateful to her. Staying home all the time, I couldn't find any for myself in this new town. Joline was thin, dark and quiet; she had a baby brother and every time she came had an amusing tale to tell about his latest escapades. Red-haired and freckled Bertha wanted to be a nurse and helped out at the hospital, delivering books to sick people. Roberta's family ran a little dairy and when she wasn't helping at the farm, she clerked for her grandparents at the little five and dime they owned nearby. Katy, forthright and tomboyish, was older than the rest of us. She was in high school and was full of talk of clothes and hairdos and boys. Those girls were busy and active, like I used to be. They had school and homework and chores at home and lots of other friends, but they found time to come and visit me, and they were good and loyal friends. Their after-school visits were my main contact with the world outside our house.

Now when I looked out in the mornings to see what kind of a day we had to rejoice in, there was snow on our mountains. The beautiful mantle of glistening white held your eyes even more than the mountains ordinarily did. You looked and couldn't stop looking at that pristine smooth loveliness against the clear blue. I begged to go to see the snow up close, so one day Daddy drove us up into the mountains. Mama piled the car full of blankets and made me put on layers of warm clothes until I could hardly move, and she filled the big old shiny steel thermos with hot cocoa. The snow looked beautiful lying softly on the trees and spread like a thick blanket on the ground. I wanted very much to get out of the car and feel the snow and walk on it and play in it, but of course I couldn't. I tried to enjoy just the looking, but after awhile I got tired of watching other children slide screaming down the white slopes, so we went back home.

We didn't go again and I didn't ask to go. I just looked at the snow on the mountains from our own windows.

Then came somebody else to keep me company and be a part of our family. One bright blue winter day I was sitting outside, well bundled up, to watch Daddy working at some task in the garage, when along the road limped a dog. He was thin and shabby and shaggy, and his feet were sore from walking, but he turned down our long driveway as if he knew exactly where he was going. That strange dog walked confidently up to me and flopped down beside my chair with a sigh, peering happily up at me through shaggy bangs, and wagging his bedraggled, curly tail. Despite the tattered appearance, those bright eyes were optimistic, courageous and cheerful. He didn't know where his next meal was coming from and couldn't remember his last one, but the little tramp didn't lower himself to beg. He'd simply rest here for a bit and see what happened. His air of coming home was so strong that we thought he must have belonged to the former owners of our house, but none of the neighbors recognized him. In fact, they said there had never been a dog living here.

Daddy's advertisement in the "Lost and Found" wasn't answered and nobody came looking for him, so I had a dog. I named my new friend "Rags" because he looked like a ragged hobo, but although a tramp in looks, Rags was always a thorough gentleman. What kind of dog he was I don't know and it didn't matter. I thought he was beautiful—and he was, too. After Mama gave him a much-needed bath, his tan and white curls were glossy and luxuriant, and his curly tail waved like a flag in the breeze. Mama trimmed the bangs hanging over his eyes so he could see his new family better, and those shining eyes brimmed with devotion.

When we lived in San Diego, we had sometimes had hobos or tramps come knocking on our door. Those were depression times and men who were out of work would wander from town to town trying to find jobs so they could send for their families. Here in San Bernardino we hadn't expected to find hobos again, but we were wrong. The major railroad lines running through the busy town made it easy for hobos to sneak rides on the boxcars, dropping off a little way out of town to try to get work in the orange orchards. We lived near the edge of town, right where the railroad starts up the long grade to the top of the mountain, so we had lots of hobos coming by wanting to work for a meal.

Mama never minded giving somebody a good meal, especially if he offered to work for it, but she didn't like those who out-and-out begged, or who were dirty or rude. If a man took his hat off and asked politely to be given a job to do in return for a meal, and if he asked if he could wash up at the faucet outside, she would fix a big plate of scrambled eggs and sliced tomatoes and toast and hand it outside to him with a tin cup of coffee. I suspect our house was marked somehow, for lots of hobos came by and almost all of them were well-behaved. After Rags came to live with us we didn't worry at all about the hobos, even when Daddy wasn't home. Rags would let most of them come right up to the back door and knock, but once in awhile he would stand out at the edge of the driveway and bark and snarl until that tramp finally slunk away. Rags could tell who was to be trusted.

Rags was part of our family now and spent most of his time amusing me. I needed some amusing, for my illness seemed to stretch on interminably into the future. And all of us could do with a little of Rags' cheerfulness, for the radio and newspapers had nothing but bad news, it seemed. The only relief in sight for the moment, the only thing to lift our spirits a bit was that, bad news or not, Christmas was coming. Mama and I were very busy making Christmas presents. When I first got sick, she had taught me to knit and crochet and embroider, and my long hours of enforced rest were brightened considerably by the slow and sure creation of pretty and useful gifts. Mama and I enjoyed those hours, sitting and sewing and talking in the cozy living room, but Daddy often thought we needed to be stirred up. After he finished his work in the yard or the garage, he would come bursting into the house on a draft of cold air, and finding us knitting companionably in the warm living room, he would say, "Get your coats on, you two. You've been cooped up in this stuffy house all day. Let's go for a ride and see the sights and get some fresh air."

Daddy had a whole new county now to roam around in. He was constantly on the lookout for new and different roads to explore and new sights to see. Sometimes he took us to see the big orange groves at the edge of town, ringed around with smudge pots ready to light if the temperature dropped to freezing. After a rain, he liked to drive out to Lytle Creek to watch the water pouring down from the mountains, sometimes so fast and furious it washed out roads and carried rocks and mud far down the valley. Daddy's favorite ride was part-way up Cajon Pass, where he could park near the train tracks. Ever since he'd been a little boy he'd loved to hear and watch the trains. Now we could sit in the car and see the long trains struggle up the steep pass very slowly, or inch down it very carefully. We'd count the locomotives. Going up there were always several for each train; it took a lot of power to haul the long trains up that steep grade. We'd count the boxcars and try to guess what was inside them and where they were going. A ride really did wake us up and make us feel better, just like Daddy thought it would.

Besides our rides, the only other place I was allowed to go was to visit the doctor. For the first time there would be no Christmas Shopping Trip for me. The little bit of Christmas shopping we did, Mama had to do by herself. She took the bus to town with my shopping list and hers, and came back tired from all that walking and loaded down with bags and boxes. Daddy always made her buy herself a nice lunch at the Tea Room, but she said it wasn't much fun all alone. Daddy bought a Christmas tree and Mama and I unpacked all the precious old ornaments. The tree looked pretty, even though it was small. When it was finished, Mama and I tried to sing the carols by ourselves, but they didn't sound quite right. It was better when we put our sweaters on and went out to stand on the front porch and look at the night sky and listen to the stars singing their own wordless Christmas carols. I hung up my stocking, although I was getting pretty big for that, and Christmas came in spite of everything. We decided to try not to listen to the news on Christmas day, but to just remember it was Christmas. With just us and the war, it was a quiet day. We had packages that came in the mail from Lewie and from George and from Thelma and from the aunts, and we had saved them to open on Christmas, so in a way they were there with us. They didn't seem quite so far away when we read their cards and opened their presents and thought about them thinking about us.

Thelma (then and always) sent the most exciting packages. That year for the first time, she sent a doll for me, and she continued to give me dolls for several Christmases, long after I should have been too old to play with dolls. The dolls Thelma sent me were very special and very different. We could never guess beforehand what they were going to be; we never knew what on earth she would do this time. Thelma had a good time looking for unusual dolls for me, and when she finally found one that tickled her fancy, she spent her spare time all the rest of the year making doll clothes. One year it was a boy doll with a wide grin and real boy clothes with flies and pockets and buttonholes. One year it was a stuffed rabbit with a complete wardrobe of old-fashioned dresses with matching pantaloons, and lacy bonnets that fit over her ears. Another year my Christmas doll was a stuffed monkey named "Fairy-Belle," with fancy, ruffled dresses and matching panties with a hole in the back for her tail to fit through.

This first year it was a cheap little baby doll that had come from the Five and Dime. In those days, a doll like that cost about a quarter, but this particular baby doll's outfits would have put a fifty-dollar doll to shame. This funny little baby doll had a whole trunkful of wonderful clothes Thelma had made for her. She had dresses of organdy and dotted Swiss with lace and ribbons and embroidery, each one with a bonnet and petticoat to match. She had a winter coat and bonnet trimmed in white fur, and a bunting to wear in the snow, and a long white christening dress. Mama had as much fun looking at those doll clothes Thelma had made as I had playing with them, and Thelma insisted it was more fun for her than for anybody.

The other present Thelma always sent at Christmas was a book. Now that I had to be quiet and not play outdoors, I was glad that I loved to read. Books were good company. I read my own books over and over again, and every week Mama took the bus to the library in town to borrow new ones for me. Mama and I liked the same kinds of books—good ones, about good people doing good things (or at least trying to). She said that reading bad books was like eating spoiled food. Bad books poison your mind like bad food poisons your body. Putting poison in your mind or your body is just plain stupid, we thought.

I got another and special book as a Christmas gift. My cousin Edgar (Uncle Edgar's son) had joined the Navy, and now he was on a submarine somewhere in the Pacific, which was a terrible worry to his parents. Cousin Edgar had sent some money to his father and asked him to buy *The Yearling* and send it to me for his Christmas present. Inside the flyleaf Uncle Edgar pasted the Christmas greeting cousin Edgar had written for me in the letter to his father. It was (and is) a good book, and a good memory.

The war began to be real. My own brothers got draft notices, but George's asthma and Lewie's badly broken arm disqualified them for military service. Edgar wasn't the only cousin to be in the war. Aunt Gladys' son Walter was in the Navy and so was Helen's husband Charles. Walter and Charles survived the war and beyond, but my cousin Edgar and all his shipmates lie in their submarine beneath the Pacific. It was a personal tragedy beyond belief for his family, a tragedy that was multiplied countless times over in the impersonal casualty lists that had begun appearing in the newspapers. We began seeing service flags in many windows now—little flags with blue or gold stars on them. Whenever a member of a family was off fighting in a war, the family would display a blue star on their house or in their window. If the star was gold, it meant that someone had died serving their country. I remembered now that some of our old photos of Grandma and Grandpa's house in Lemon Grove showed a service flag with three stars. That was years ago, during the First World War, when three of their sons were fighting in that war. Now, in this new war, some of our relatives had blue stars in their windows again, and one had a gold star. I thought about that gold star for cousin Edgar in the window of his home, and all the other stars on other houses across the country. I wanted my old pepper tree to sit in and wonder about things, but I didn't have it, so I sat in my chair with Rags' head on my knee and wondered about everything.

With the reality of war came the understanding that death was real—something that not only could but would happen to people you knew and loved, and even to yourself as well. Death wasn't merely missing people, like I missed Grandma and Grandpa, it was knowing they weren't anywhere in the world with you any more. Shortly after Grandpa died we had visited a park where there was a lovely fountain. I was amazed to see coins sparkling in the water at the bottom of the fountain and asked Mama about them. "Oh," she smiled, "it's a wishing well. If you throw in a coin and make a wish, it's supposed to come true." I begged a coin and made my wish, but I didn't tell Mama what I was going to wish for. Here, I thought, seemed to be the way out of my private worry. Closing my eyes and tossing my penny I made my silent and fierce demand, "I wish Mama and Daddy will never die." Now that I was older and wiser, I looked back scornfully at that incident as from a great stretch of years, and thought what a silly baby I had been to try to cheat death with a wish. I knew now that it couldn't come true. And it didn't.

The war made itself felt in many ways, even in our quiet house. Daddy worried about the gasoline rations, while Mama pored over the food ration books—how much meat, how much sugar. She often had to stand in long lines at the butcher shop and then had to be grateful for whatever kind of meat the butcher had. There were air raid drills with the siren blaring out in the night. Never quite certain if it were real or just a drill, you would hurry to turn out lights and pull down the blackout shades so no crack of light could shine out to show enemy planes the way to the air base. That siren was even more awful in the night than the fire alarm had been. Hearing the fire alarm, you knew help would soon be on the way. Hearing the air raid siren, you couldn't be certain bombs wouldn't be dropping from the night sky, like they were across the sea.

Mama worked with neighbors to collect old clothes and things for "Bundles for Britain" to be sent to England to help people where the bombs really were dropping out of the sky. Mama washed the clothes and I helped sort and mend and pack them carefully. We sent them off, hoping they would reach England and not be sunk in the ocean. We conserved everything we were supposed to conserve and saved tinfoil and rubber. We grew our Victory garden and bought our Victory bonds, and tried to believe that life would ever be carefree again. Casualty lists in the newspapers grew longer and longer and the winter grew darker and drearier.

After Christmas my school lessons at home began again. We studied current events and followed the war carefully. Another kind of lessons began for me now: music lessons. Mama and Daddy bought a little violin for me and found a music teacher who would come to the house to teach me. All at once a new door opened, a grand big door with wonderful things inside—just like the door to the library when I learned to read so long ago. I had never thought much about music before. Of course, I had learned how to read music at school, and I liked to sing the songs we learned there and at Sunday School, and I loved the old Christmas carols. But I was completely ignorant of the glories of classical music. At the instigation of my violin teacher, I began to listen to concerts on the radio and to collect records of great music. Uncle Edgar (a fine pianist as well as an artist) had a large collection of classical records and generously sent me his duplicates. Mama haunted the Goodwill Store for used records, and all three of us found a great deal of pleasure in listening to the wonderful music to revive our spirits after hearing the news broadcasts. The winter dragged on, and I learned my lessons and practiced my music, we listened to the news and waited for the air raid siren.

It sometimes seemed, when the news was all bad, that it was wrong of us to enjoy what we had when so many people had everything blown away. Maybe it was wrong to laugh when so many people were crying. We began feeling sad and worried all the time until Mama saw how down in the dumps we were getting. She scolded us in her own gentle way, and made us realize that we must take the good with the bad. It was our job to keep ourselves strong and useful in whatever way we could, for that was the only way to prevent evil from swallowing up the world. That there was truly evil loose in the world was becoming clearer as time went on. It was amazing to us that real people could follow the leadership of such a person as Hitler. Daddy joined the long line at the library to get on a waiting list for *Mein Kampf*, but even after reading that horrifying book, he still could scarcely understand how Hitler had become such a power in his own country and in the world. By this time, we knew it wasn't going to be a short or easy war. This was the "war to end all wars," but would it?

Daddy was too old to fight a war, but he served his country in another way. Although he was retired, his long experience in the fire department was desperately needed. He went back to work, this time as a fire chief working for the Army at the nearby base. Now, just like before he retired, he was going to work and coming home, and Mama was worrying. It wasn't fires in people's homes or stores that he helped put out now—it was fires at the Army base and fires in crashed airplanes. And those were terrible. Sometimes Daddy would come home with a white face and shaking hands. He couldn't eat any supper and Mama would fix him a cup of coffee and sit at the kitchen table with him. He would lay his glasses down on the table and rub his eyes with his hands and mutter in a broken voice, "They're rushing too fast. They're sending those kids up before they're trained." Mama would reach out and take his hand in hers and not say a word.

That winter was a long one. We all got very tired of darkness and bad news and wondered if it would ever end. The bright spots—Rags, and music, and books, and friends—helped some, but there were times when looking ahead I could see nothing except illness and isolation and war and air raid sirens. We tried to keep busy. When there was nothing else to do but worry, Daddy would bring from the garage a box of things from the old house in San Diego for us to unpack. Those were things we wanted to keep, but things we hadn't needed in the house right away. It was interesting to dig into the big boxes and find things you had forgotten about. Sometimes we set aside things for "Bundles for Britain" or for the Goodwill Store, and sometimes we threw things in the trash. Sometimes we found treasures that we could take out and enjoy right now.

That's the way it was with Daddy's old Navy trunk. In it were important things that Mama and Daddy had kept for a long time. There was Thelma's fine white baby dress and George's baby shoes and Junior's silver baby spoon and my baby-size gold bracelet. There was the little kewpie doll that had decorated the radiator cap of Daddy's jitney bus the first time he picked Mama up. There was the book he gave her before they were married, *Trail of the Lonesome Pine*. There was the doll he gave her the first Christmas after they were married, just for fun. Even older than those was a little cut glass top hat and a shoe (I thought it looked like Cinderella's glass slipper). In Grandma's girlhood those pretty glass containers were kept on the bureau to put matches in and to collect hair from your comb. The ladies kept their hair combings to make into "rats," which they would wear underneath their own hair in front to puff up their pompadours. That little glass shoe and hat had traveled long ago in a covered wagon from Kansas to Oregon on the Oregon Trail.

Mama told me how her mother, who was fifteen years old at that time, had ridden her pinto pony the whole way from Kansas to Oregon. It was hard for me to picture my Grandma doing that, but she had loved horses and she was a brave girl. There was one night on the Trail when all their horses had disappeared. The men were worried that maybe Indians had stolen them. Because my Grandma had made friends with all the horses, they let her—a young girl—walk out onto the prairies alone, over the hills and hollows, calling those horses. They hoped that if the Indians were lurking around, they wouldn't feel threatened by a girl. They hoped that if the horses had only strayed away, they would come to her when she called them. That girl that was later my Grandma did find the horses (for they had only strayed away) and so the wagon train was able to go on. I thought that was a brave thing for a girl to do, not knowing if there were Indians waiting behind the bushes ready to shoot her.

In the trunk with the other things was a dress that Grandma had worn when she was a young woman. It was black silk and was made by hand. It had a high collar and fancy ruffling and tucks, and it was lined with rows of corset stays caught down on each edge with fine little stitches. The garment was so tiny that it was hard to believe that a grown woman could have worn it, but Grandma was tiny—almost as tiny as my other Grandma in Illinois. In the trunk, too was the beautiful quilt that my Illinois Grandma had made for me.

There too was a coverlet that Thelma had made when I was born. She was only thirteen years old when she pieced and stitched those twelve beautiful quilt blocks to make a crib cover for me. The "Sunbonnet Girl" was an adorable little character from a series of books for children, and that was the pattern Thelma used to make the blocks. Each little-girl figure was made of only four simple pieces. There was a flared dress shape, a bonnet in profile, a round shoe below the dress, and an arm shape appliquéd onto the dress. Thelma cut each dress of a different figured cloth and each bonnet of matching plain material. She basted the edges smooth and appliquéd the pieces on plain white muslin squares with tiny stitches. Then she used her imagination to decorate each dress and bonnet differently. Some had lace or rickrack around dress and bonnet, some had a row of embroidered flowers. One even had a tiny pocket with a handkerchief corner poking out. That coverlet was a wonderful piece of work, especially for a thirteen-year-old. After Thelma had made all the blocks, Mama sewed them together with bands of flowered material around each one and around the edge. Mama had used it as a crib cover when I was very little. Now that we had unpacked it from the trunk, I looked at that darling coverlet again and asked Mama to let me use it for a bedspread now. She washed it and ironed it and sewed a ruffle on the sides to make it big enough to use on my bed. It made one of the most delightful bedspreads I have ever seen, and that precious coverlet was destined to become a treasured wall hanging much later.

The only other bright spot in that long dreary winter was Thelma's unexpected return to us. For her, I think it was a sad return. For me, it was joyous. We all went to the train station to meet her, and Daddy welcomed her with open arms and never once said, "I told you so." He didn't say anything at all, except to call her "Sary-Jane," which was his pet name for his oldest girl. He just hugged her hard and patted her on the back and brought her and her trunk home. Thelma talked alone with Mama and they both cried a little. Mama wouldn't be angry in front of Thelma, but later with Daddy, she could be about as angry as Mama ever got. "That man," she snapped, and then stopped because I was there.

My school lessons, my music lessons, and my books were filling my days with learning. Now, along with all my other lessons, Thelma began to teach me to sew—another enduring pleasure for me. She picked out a pattern for dresses for us to make just alike and bought the material—red with white dots. She cut out the pieces and showed me how to baste them together; then she sewed the seams on Mama's new sewing machine. Mama had an electric sewing machine now. This new one didn't have a treadle that Mama had to pump with her feet, and it didn't have iron curlicues that I had to dust, like the old sewing machine had. After Thelma sewed the pieces together on the machine, she and I sewed the hems and the buttons by hand. When the dresses were finished we wore them on Sundays and even Daddy thought they were pretty and said we looked nice.

It was good to have Thelma living with us again, but it wasn't long before she got a job at the Army base where Daddy worked. She got an apartment for herself and moved out of our house, but this time nobody was angry or crying. And this time she would be living near enough to visit often. Thelma was just going off to live in her own place and try again to do what she wanted to do, if she could figure out what that was.

The time came when Daddy's experience in the fire department and with airplane crashes was needed at another airfield many miles away, and then we had to face moving again. That was a blow, for we were tired of packing and unpacking. We were tired of changes. We had our almost new house and our pretty yard and Mama's roses and Daddy's chickens. We had made friends here and were just getting used to the new town. Mama hated to be uprooted again and she hated to try to find new friends and a new doctor for me and a new school teacher and music teacher. Mama hated the idea of living in government "housing" as we would have to do. Most of all, she hated for Daddy to work on more of those terrible airplane fires. But she loved him more than she hated all those things, so she just got busy and packed and tried not to say very much about it. There was a war and people did what they had to do and tried not to complain.

Daddy didn't sell our house, because we wanted to come back to it after—well, whenever we could. I wondered if it would all be there when we returned and what would happen to it in the meantime. Would the roses blossom sweetly in the morning dew? Would the pine trees still sing in the fall wind? Would the climbing rose on the front porch shower its scarlet petals down on a fine summer morning? Would the mountains still peer in the window with their crown of winter snows? If they did, would we be here to enjoy it? Uncertainty had become a fact of life.

We had no idea what we were going to find when we got where we were going. Daddy said we would live in "housing" and described rows of buildings built all alike right on the Army base. There would be no grass, no flowers, no trees, because the base was very new and there had been no time to plant things. In fact, there wouldn't be very much grass, flowers, or trees anywhere around, because the base was in a desert where there was only flatness and dirt. And oil wells instead of trees. It all sounded pretty dreary. We had no way of knowing what we were soon to realize: the beauty of desert sunsets, the delight of seeing far off to a distant horizon, the immensity of cloudless skies, the interesting activity of a military base, and the friendliness of a motley conglomeration of civilians and military personnel thrown together by the common cause of national defense. As for missing our friends, we soon remembered that letters can be written to old friends and new friends collected like jewels on an endless string. Mama found that house plants could substitute for her roses, and I found that books and music were everywhere.

Everywhere, too, were servicemen and women, flags waving, and airplanes flying or sometimes not. Daddy was caught up again in the horror of crashes and fires that were beyond the limits of his control. His job was to train firefighters. He took raw recruits and incompetents and made them into tough crews. They were very good, but they couldn't achieve miracles. There were still those bad times when he came home furious or helpless with despair. "It's darkest before the dawn," the saying goes, and we wondered about that. It was dark enough right now—was it going to be even darker? How dark was darkest? And would there be a dawn? Grandpa had said, "This is the day which the Lord hath made; let us rejoice and be glad in it." What was there to rejoice in now? Could we be glad in a day when terrible things were happening in the world? Could we rejoice when there was illness and death and isolation and estrangement and anger and hate and war? To all these questions we didn't know the answers. But the answers were there.

Spring came again. Roses bloomed.

AFTERTHOUGHTS

L ooking back from my vantage point of years, I see now that I had as a child what all children need most: a life structure that was solid and reliable, people who were always there, a foundation that could be depended upon. Childhood is the time for blessed security and sameness, comfort and warmth. Growing up, whether it happens suddenly or gradually, is the child's understanding that there is no true security and nothing ever stays the same. For me, that understanding began slowly with the normal and gradual breaking up of the close family circle. At the time I knew only that I wanted to go back, to have everything be exactly like it had been. Given time to sort things out, I saw that change is everywhere. Change is constant and ongoing and inexorable. People come and go and even die. The vast mountains to which we lift up our eyes are changing and evolving little by infinitesimal little. Even the unchangeable stars change—not while we watch, not within our lifetime—but nevertheless continually changing and becoming their destiny.

My transition from childhood began not with one single event, but with a gradual awakening to the reality of change, comfortable or uncomfortable. As surely as night follows day or seedtime follows harvest, change will take place. Each individual makes his own way, choosing his paths and detours as he goes. Each choice determines at last whether the result is to move slowly and painfully ahead to adulthood or to regress to continued immaturity, to become something larger or to return shrinking to the warmth of the womb, to employ fortitude or to whine and snivel, to take joy in tortuous growth or to settle for stagnation. Beginning to grow up, I discovered the only security was inside myself, the only dependable foundation was my own soul, and it was only the goodness and values which I was taught that are reliable. As a frightened child I cried and wished and clung to the past. As a growing adult I could peer into the unknowable future with hope and gratitude, saying, "This is the day. . . I will rejoice and be glad."

THE END